CHAPTER 3 52
Google Docs 52
The Benefits of Google Docs 53
How To Access the Google Docs 55
Google Docs User Interface 56
Create Folders on Google Docs 60
Share Documents on Google Docs 60
Print Documents from Google Docs 61
Comparing Google Docs and Microsoft Word 62
Functions and features of Microsoft Word 63
Google Docs Functions and Features 65

CHAPTER 4 67
Google Sheets 67
How To Access Google Sheet 69
Google Sheet User Interface 70
How To Create Google Sheet 71
Importing Data into Google Sheets 72
Formatting Files on Google Sheet 74
How To Share Files on Google Sheet 76
How To Print on Google Sheet 78
Basic Formulas on Google Sheet 79
Google Sheets SUM function 80
MAX & MIN functions 81

Google Workspace 2023 Handbook

A Quick Guide to Help Seniors & Beginners Get Started & Master All of Google's Collaborative Apps: Gmail, Drive, Sheets, Docs, Slides, Forms, & Other Useful Tools

Leonard A. McFizz

© Copyright 2021 Leonard A. McFizz. All rights reserved.

The content contained within this book may not be reproduced, duplicated or transmitted without direct written permission from the author or the publisher.

Under no circumstances will any blame or legal responsibility be held against the publisher, or author, for any damages, reparation, or monetary loss due to the information contained within this book. Either directly or indirectly. You are responsible for your own choices, actions, and results.

Legal Notice:
This book is copyright protected. This book is only for personal use. You cannot amend, distribute, sell, use, quote or paraphrase any part, or the content within this book, without the consent of the author or publisher.

Table of content

INTRODUCTION ....

CHAPTER 1 ....
- Google Apps...
- Signing Up for a Google Account...................
- Accessing Google Apps ....
  - Google Apps for Business ....
  - Google Apps for Developers ....
- Install Google Apps on Your Smartphone ....
- How To Change Your Google Profile Picture ......
- Change Personal Information on Google Account
- Manage Your Google Privacy and Security Setting
  - Google Apps Covered In This Book..................

CHAPTER 2 ....
- Google Drive ....
  - The Benefits of Using Google Drive...............
- Accessing Google Drive 3
- Uploading Files Into Google Drive .... 3!
- How To Create Files on Google Drive 40
- Tools On Google Drive.................................. 42
- Copy A File on Google Drive 44
- How To Use Google Drive Offline Mode 46
- One Drive and Google Drive 49

Google Sheets IF function 83
COUNT & COUNTA 86
Calculating Averages on Google Sheet 88
Working with Functions and Percentage 89
How to Create Charts and Graphs in Google Sheet
.... 92

Excel Vs Google Sheet 94

CHAPTER 5 98

Google Slides 98

How To Access Google Slides 98

Creating a New Presentation................................... 99

Google Slide User Interface 100
The Menu Bars.. 101
Setting Up your Slide 103
Adding More Slides... 104
How to Insert Text on Your Slide 106
How to Format Your Slide................................... 106
Import Files to Google Slides.............................. 108
How to Apply Transition and Animation on Google Slides.. 108
How to Apply Animation in Slides 110
How to Share Presentation on Google Slides..... 111
How to Publish your Presentation on Google Slide
.... 112

- Google Slide Vs Microsoft PowerPoint 113
- CHAPTER 6 115
  - Google Forms 115
    - How To Access Google Forms 117
    - Google Form User Interface 117
    - How to Create a Google Form 118
  - Question Types 121
    - Importing a Question 122
  - Sending And Sharing Google Forms 125
    - Using a Template 126
- CHAPTER 7 128
  - GOOGLE KEEP 128
    - Access Google Keep 129
    - Google Keep Interface 130
    - To create a note 131
    - To Edit a note 131
    - Making a List 132
    - To Make a Sketch 132
  - Making a New Note with an Image 133
    - How to Organize Your Different Notes 134
  - Add Labels 134
  - Pin Notes 136
  - To-Do Lists 137

- Mark by Color 138
  - How to Share Notes and Collaborate on Google Keep 139
  - Archives and Reminder.. 140
  - How to Export your Google Keep Note 143
  - Google Keep Chrome Extension 144
  - How to Disable Chrome Extensions.................... 145
- CHAPTER 8 147
  - Google Photos 147
    - How to Access Google Photos 148
  - Google Photo Interface 150
    - Upload Photos to Google Photos 152
    - Download Google Photos 153
    - Creating an Album on Google Photo 155
    - Share Photos and Videos on Google Photo........ 155
    - Create a Shared Album on Google Photo........... 157
    - Back Up Photos with Google Photo.................... 157
    - Google Photo on Mobile Devices 158
  - Google Photos Vs Gallery 159
- CHAPTER 9 161
  - Google Calendar And Gmail 161
    - How To Access Google Calendar 163
    - Add An Event to Your Calendar 165
    - Editing and Deleting an Event 166

Delete an event 167

    To Create a Google Calendar 168

    Add Tasks and Reminders on Google Calendar .. 169

    Tips for Google Calendars 170

Gmail 174

    How to Create Gmail Account 175

    Gmail Interface 177

    Sending and Receiving Mails 179

    How to Print Email Messages 180

    Creating a Filter 182

    Gmail Tips 184

CHAPTER 10 187

Other Google Apps 187

    Google Meet 187

    Google Hangouts 188

    Google Chat 189

    Google Classroom 190

    Google Contact 191

    Google Maps 192

    Manipulating the map 193

    Google Chrome 195

INTRODUCTION

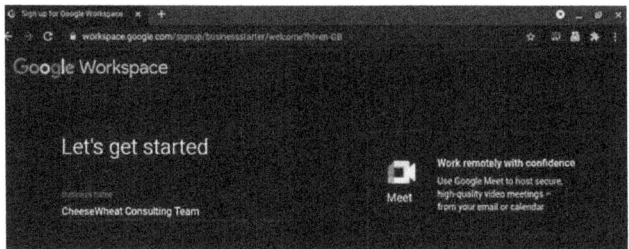

Google is way more than a search engine. The full list of services it offers is almost as mind-blowing as the number of fast searches it conducts almost every nanosecond in a 24 hours' time range. Other services include applications for word processing; working with spreadsheets; creating presentations; reading, writing, and storing your email, and scheduling appointments and meetings. Google has been able to bring communication, productivity, and collaboration tools right to your Web browser.

From being just a search engine, Google transitioned to providing great services for its users. With Google Applications in vogue now and then, a person with excellent knowledge of how to use these tools wouldn't be able to use every one of them at the same time. I believe every user should remain updated so as not to be left behind in this ever-changing digital era.

On Google's client computing infrastructure, some web apps and services make up Google Workspace. The apps that are part of Google Workspace include the Gmail email service, Google Drive online storage, the productivity apps Google Docs, Google Sheets, and Slides, the Google Keep note-taking app, the Google Forms app for creating forms, distributing them, and collecting responses, as well as many communication apps like Google Meet and Google Chat.

The free services that Google offers to users in return for some of their data are well-recognized worldwide. Customers can use the Google search engine, Gmail email service, and Google Hangouts chat and video conferencing service without paying a fee.

Google Workspace, in comparison, charges a monthly price for each user and is geared toward businesses. If you are acquainted with all Google apps, it is a great tool since it connects them and makes them simpler to use if you deal with Google products. I also enjoy how it combines all Google productivity and collaboration tools into a single package for access by several teams. Along with Google Docs, Sheets, Forms, and Slides, the list of applications also includes Gmail, Hangouts, Calendar, Drive, and Sites.

Many of the applications and services offered by Google Workspace are the same as those that are freely accessible to and often used by individual customers; however, Google Workspace bundles them into a complete package that offers additional features and improved capabilities. For instance, Google Workspace gives more capacity on Google Drive, administrative tools for setting up and maintaining user accounts, and the ability for a business to utilize its domain for email addresses.

I choose Google Workspace because it facilitates time efficiency and considerably simplifies my work by making organizing and processing data easier and quicker. Sharing and storing files is one feature I enjoy. You don't need a lot of expertise to figure it out since it is so simple to use and intuitive. Due to how easy it is to share links and information with others, it is quite engaging.

Google offers a lot more than a search engine as its services are every user's go-to tool in today's world. In this book, we will be covering some of the tools and services offered by Google. This will expose you to numerous opportunities you can find on Google that would aid you in your day-to-day activities.

CHAPTER 1

Google Apps

What Are Google Apps?

Google Applications are a collection of web-based programs and files that can run and properly execute in a web browser. These applications could be either web-based or as a collaborative Software as a Service (SaaS) solution that customizes the Google platform and brand for businesses of all sizes, including large enterprises.

Google Apps include a personalized start page (iGoogle), communication tools (Gmail, Google Talk, and Google Calendar), productivity tools (Google Docs: texts, spreadsheets, and presentations), and Google Sites. Google Sites allows users to create and host their own websites (to develop web pages).

Files may be appropriately stored and maintained by Google in several versions. With Google Apps, sharing a certain document or folder is as easy as allowing someone access, which might be for everyone or just a select group of individuals. In general, it aids in the dissemination of information.

The same resources and infrastructure that support Google's basic services are also available for Google Apps. It claims capabilities like administrative assistance, other business support, and 100% availability, all of which are specifically included in the Google Apps Service Level Agreement (SLA).

The following categories apply to both commercial and private Google apps. They are:

- Google Apps (free): This package contains Google Docs, Gmail, Google Calendar, and Google Sites.
- Google Apps for Education: For students who wish to utilize its tools, Google provides free educational services.

- Google Apps for Business: This product has a premium edition and offers Web-based collaboration capabilities.

Signing Up for a Google Account

Creating a Google account is straightforward. You'll need to provide some basic information, like your name, age, and location.

Once you have successfully created and verified your account, you'll be able to easily access other Google services like Gmail, Google Docs, Google Calendar, and many others services.

Accessing Gmail requires a Google account as well since it is one of the numerous services that Google offers to registered customers. Additionally, because creating a Gmail account is a requirement for signing up, you would have to do so. This means that anytime you sign in to

Gmail, your Google account is also automatically logged in.

To create a Google account, do the following:

Step 1: Go to www.google.com.

Step 2: Select the Sign-in button in the top-right corner of the page.

Step 3: Tap Create an account.

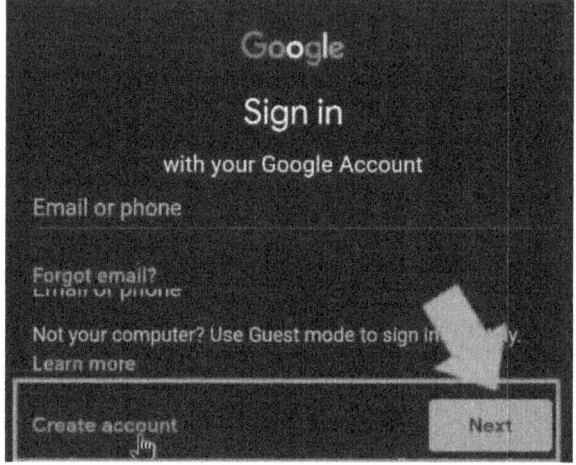

Step 4: The sign-up form will appear. Then, go through the necessary directions and enter the required information.

Step 5: Enter your phone number.

Note: Google will send a verification code in the form of an OTP(one-time password) to your device. This would help you complete the sign-up process.

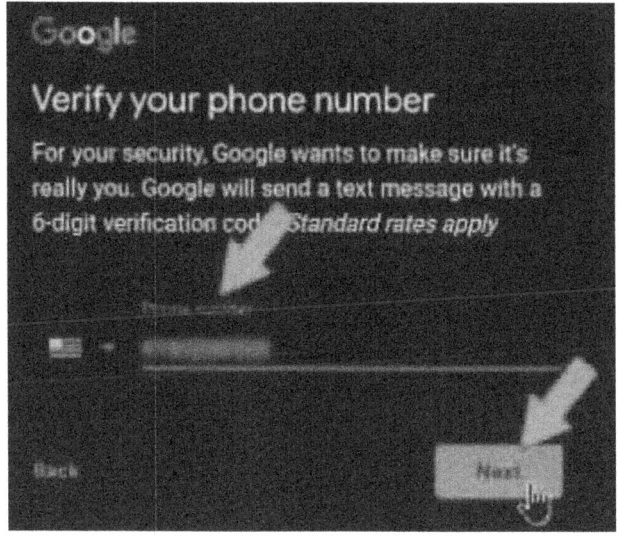

Step 6: Enter the verification code sent to your phone and Select Verify.

Step 7: A personal information page will appear. Follow the directions and enter your information, including your birth date and gender.

Step 8: Review Google's Terms of Service and Privacy Policy, then Select I agree.

Accessing Google Apps

You can sign into Google apps and even third-party apps and services with your Google account. You don't necessarily have to remember the individual usernames and passwords for each account. To access Google apps:

1. Go to an app.

2. Tap Sign in with Google on the Sign-in page.

3. Log in with Google.

Tip: If you trust a third-party app, you should choose to allow permission. You may see what kind of access to your account and which Google services a third party has.

Recall that you can only access "**Manage third-party access**" if you allow access to third-party applications. This is how:

1. Go to the Security section of your Google Account.

2. Under "Third-party apps with account access," choose Manage third-party access.

3. Tap the app or service you want to review.

List Of All Google Apps

Google apps range from system apps to web apps. It varies all round but here is the list of Google Applications in different categories:

Search Tools

- Google Search
- Google Alerts
- Google Assistant

- Google Books
- Google Dataset Search
- Google Flights
- Google Images
- Google Shopping
- Google Travel
- Google Videos

Advertising Services

- Google Ads
- AdMob
- Google AdSense
- Google Ad Manager
- Google Marketing Platform
- Google Tag Manager

Communication and Publishing tool

- Blogger

- FeedBurner
- Google Chat
- Google Collections
- Google Classroom
- Google Currents
- Google Duo
- Google Fonts
- Google Groups
- Google Meet
- Google Voice

Productivity tools

- Gmail
- Google Account
- Google Calendar
- Google Charts
- Google Domains

- Google Docs Editors
- Google Docs
- Google Sheets
- Google Slides
- Google Drawings
- Google Forms
- Google Sites
- Google Keep
- Google Drive
- Google Jamboard
- Google Translate

Google Apps for Business

Google apps have transitioned in such a way that businesses also can make good use of them. These are some of the google apps mostly used by businesses today:

- Google Workspace – a suite of web applications for businesses, education providers, and nonprofits that include customizable versions of several Google products accessible through a custom domain name. Services include Gmail, Google Contacts, Google Calendar, Google Docs Editors, Google Sites, Google Meet, Google Chat, Google Cloud Search, and more. One Google workspace exclusive product is Google Vault.
- Google My Business
- Google Tables (beta)

Google Apps for Developers

Developers are not left behind in the place of Google applications. Here are a few apps they make use of in writing a few codes and setting up some programming. They include:

- Accelerated Mobile Pages (AMP)

- Google App Engine
- Google Developers
- Dart
- Flutter
- Go (programming language)
- OpenSocial
- Google PageSpeed Tools
- Google Web Toolkit
- Google Search Console Sitemap
- Gerrit
- Googletest
- Bazel
- FlatBuffers
- Protocol Buffers
- Shaderc
- Google Guava

- Google Closure Tools

- Google Collaboratory

Install Google Apps on Your Smartphone

To install Google Applications on your smartphone, you don't need to do so much. Google has made it easy for users to get easily acquainted with their applications. These are a few steps you could take to install Google Applications on your smartphone:

1. Open Google Play Store on your smartphone.

2. On the right side, tap the profile icon.

3. Tap Manage apps & device and then tap Manage.

4. Choose the apps you are to install

Note: If you can't locate the app. Look at the top of the page and click on Installed and then Not installed.

5. Select Install or Enable.

How To Change Your Google Profile Picture

Your Google profile picture is constant as long as you make use of Google services such as Gmail, Google Chrome, Google Meet, and even the Google Play store on Android. You can easily change your Google profile picture by changing your Gmail profile picture. This is because your Gmail profile picture is the same as your Google Profile picture.

1. Launch Gmail on your computer.
2. Choose your profile image from the menu that appears in the upper right-hand corner of the page.
3. Choose the Manage Your Account option from the menu.
4. On the page for your Google Account, choose the "Personal info" option.

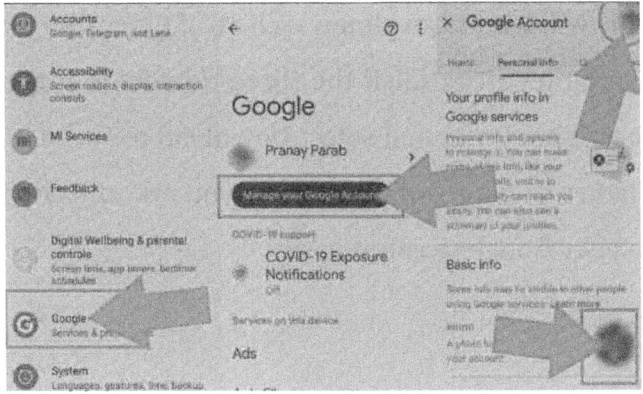

5. Under "Profile," choose your current profile picture.
6. Follow the on-screen guide to choose or take a new profile photo.
7. Tap Set Profile Photo.

Note: If you want to select a picture from your previous list of uploaded profile pictures, you can click on the three-dot icon in the top-right corner of the Change Profile Picture dialog box. Then select the previous profile pictures.

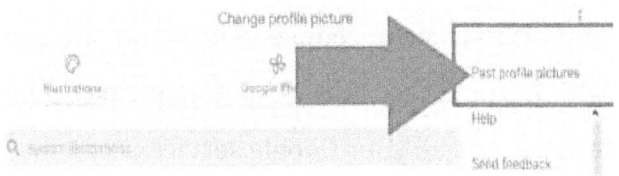

27

This will lead to an album archive of older Google profile pictures. Click the three-dots icon in the top-right corner and select Download to save the picture to your computer. Now you can upload it to your Google account easily.

Change Personal Information on Google Account

After creating a Google account whether it be for personal or business use, you will find out that your Google account name is used by default across many of the Google services you make use of. This includes Gmail, YouTube, Drive, Photos, and more.

However, you can change or update your account for some Google services individually. These could be your account name or even phone number. It's easier to change your name on your Google Account so that it automatically gets updated across all your Google services.

1. Go to your Google account in a web browser.

2. Sign-in to your account.

3. Choose Personal Info from the left vertical menu.

4. From the right side of your name, select the right-facing arrow.

5. Enter your new first and/or last name in the given fields.

6. Select Save immediately after you're done with the necessary changes.

Note: If after going through the aforementioned steps to change your personal information but it still turns up, you could try clearing your browser cache and cookies.

Manage Your Google Privacy and Security Settings

Google is a business that benefits from using user data. It utilizes information about your activities and interests to target advertisements, create new services, create algorithms, and carry out other commercial operations.

As long as you use Google's services, it's almost difficult to prevent data collecting, but you can easily set certain restrictions on what information Google may collect and how it can use it.

Utilizing Google's privacy settings is the first step in imposing constraints. With the help of some recent improvements, you can alter these privacy settings to fit your preferences. These consist of;

1. On your computer, Open Chrome.

2. At the top right corner of the page click More.

3. Select Settings.

4. Tap on Privacy and security and then choose your settings.

Note:

- To control how Chrome handles content and permissions for a site, Select Site settings.

- To delete information from your browsing activity, like your history, cookies, or saved passwords, click Clear browsing data.

- To control how Chrome handles cookies and tracking, click on Cookies and then select other site data.

- To manage safe browsing and protection, Tap Security.

Google Apps Covered In This Book

Gmail, Google Talk, Google Calendar, Google Docs, Google Videos, and Google Cloud Connect are just a few of the Google services and user management features that are made easier to use by Google Applications.

Not all of Google's services are discussed in this book, although there are a good number of them. They consist of:

Google Drive, Google Slides, Google Sheets, Google Docs, Google Forms, Google Calendar, Google Keep, Google Photos, Gmail, Google Meet, Google Hangouts, Google Chat, Google Classroom, Google Contact, Google Maps, and Google Chrome.

CHAPTER 2

Google Drive

WHAT IS GOOGLE DRIVE?

One of the most widely used cloud storage options nowadays is Google Drive. Consider the benefits of storing your data online if you've never utilized a cloud-based storage service like Google Drive. Drive does away with the need to email or save a file to a USB drive since data may be accessible from any computer with an Internet connection. And because Drive enables file sharing, collaborating with others is made much simpler.

When you use Google Drive, you may upload files to the cloud for free and then access those files from any location in the world. You may also generate documents, spreadsheets, presentations, and other sorts of files by making use of free web-based apps that are accessible via Google Drive.

The Benefits of Using Google Drive

#1: Easy-to-use interface

You are met with a list of your most recent papers at the top of the screen, a list of all of your folders right below that, and a straightforward navigation bar on the left that allows you to:

- Create a new document.
- View shared folders between computers.
- View documents shared outside of your drive.
- See recent, starred, or deleted documents.

All these happen in just one click.

#2: Microsoft Office compatible

Let's imagine you're all set to start utilizing Google Drive, but everyone else in your office is still stuck on Microsoft Office. None of the parties concerned will be negatively impacted as a result of this.

You can access documents created in Microsoft Word or Excel in Google Drive, and you can also convert documents created in Google Drive into versions compatible with Microsoft Office.

As a result, you and your other team members will have no difficulty opening and using these files, as will you. Google Drive makes it incredibly simple to share files with other people, including your coworkers.

#3: Share your files using a custom link

- On Google Drive, every single file and folder has its sharing link, as well as the capability to define who has access to that link:
- You have the ability to modify the kind of permission you provide to everyone who has access to your custom link by clicking on the pencil symbol.

Notice that this not only enables your staff to make necessary adjustments, but it also prevents the document from being accidentally altered by a third party that is not affiliated with your business.

Also, this method is applicable to any kind of file that you could be working on.

#4: Store videos, PDFs, presentations, and photos

You may save documents of varying dimensions and lengths using Google Drive. You then have the option to either share them with others or keep them stored securely and secretly in your Drive; the decision is yours to make.

You can also store files that are attached to emails directly to Drive, which enables you to maintain an organized collection of crucial attachments and place them precisely where you need them.

#5: Access your documents from anywhere in the world

Just like with OneDrive, your Google Drive is accessible anywhere you have an internet connection. As long as you can sign into Google, you'll be able to access all your documents and files.

The Drive app also allows you to synchronize all of your devices, which means that everything you are working on in Drive on one device is available on all of your other devices. You may be asking, in light of all these wonderful advantages of utilizing Google Drive, whether or not there are any negatives to doing so.

And, as is the case with most things, there are, albeit thankfully there are only half as many disadvantages as there are benefits.

Accessing Google Drive

You should be aware of how to access Google Drive files from anyplace if you often use devices other than your home computer or work remotely. You can view your files using any browser on any device once they have synchronized.

How to access Google Drive from a web browser (any device):

- Open up any web browser, then go to Google Drive.

How to access Google Drive from a desktop computer:

- Install Google Drive for Mac or PC, then open the Google Drive folder on your desktop

If you don't specify a different folder while installing Google Drive, the folder will be stored in the computer's default directory.

Uploading Files Into Google Drive

- On your computer, go to drive.google.com.

- At the top left, click New.

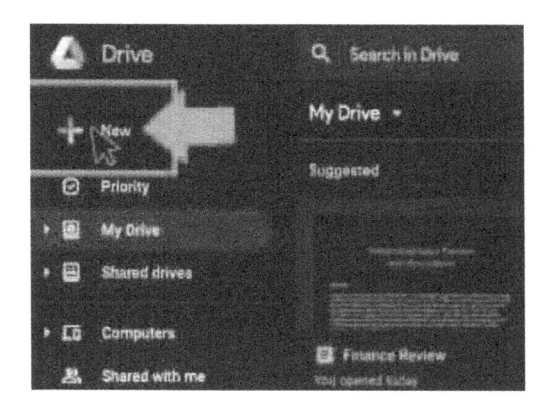

- Click on file upload.

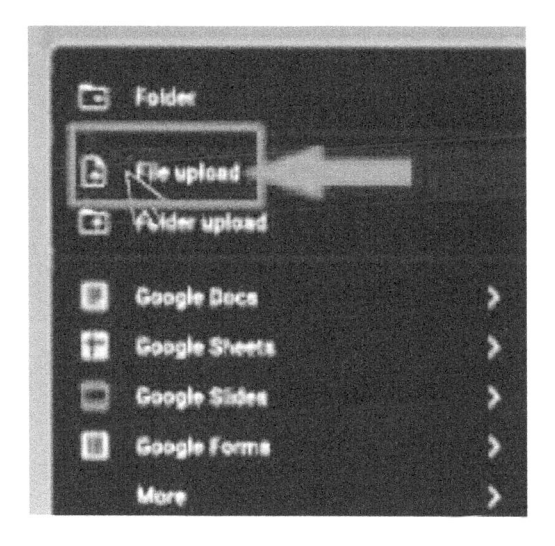

- Choose the file you want to upload

How To Create Files on Google Drive

Along with storing your files, Google Drive also offers productivity tools that let you create, organize, and share documents. Some aspects of Google Drive's programs could be recognizable if you've ever used a suite like Microsoft Office. The sorts of files you can deal with, for instance, are comparable to those that can be produced by some Microsoft Office products.

The following file formats are available for creation and sharing on Google Drive:

- For creating letters, flyers, essays, and other text-based projects, use **Google Docs** (similar to Microsoft Word documents)
- **Google Sheets**: For archiving and classifying data (similar to Microsoft Excel workbooks)

- For making slide displays, use **Google Slides** (similar to Microsoft PowerPoint presentations)
- **Google Drawings** is a tool for producing simple vector images or diagrams. Google Forms is a tool for gathering and organizing data.

To create a new file:

Locate the New button on Google Drive, click it, then pick the kind of file you wish to create. We'll use Google Docs for our example to start a new document.

Your browser will open a new tab with your new file in it. In the upper-left corner, find and choose **Untitled document**.

You'll see the Rename dialog box. Click **OK** after giving your file a name.

Your file's name will change. The document will be instantly saved to your Google Drive, where you can view it whenever you want. Simply double-click the file to reopen it.

You may have noticed that your files don't have a Save button. This is due to the autosave feature of Google Drive, which instantly and automatically saves your edited files.

Tools On Google Drive

There are some Google Workspace productivity tools available with your UIndy Google Account. This article offers a summary of common tools available with links to more information. Of the tools listed below, all are available in your web browser with no additional required software needed.

- **Google Docs**

With Google Docs you can create and edit text documents. For more information navigate to Google's information about Google Docs.

- **Google Sheets**

With Google Sheets, you can create and edit spreadsheets. For more information navigate to Google's information about Google Sheets.

- **Google Slides**

With Google Slides you can build presentations. For more information navigate to Google's information about Google Slides.

- **Google Forms**

With Google Forms, you can create and analyze surveys. For more information navigate to Google's information about Google Forms.

Copy A File on Google Drive

How to transfer files in Google Drive is one Google Drive feature that many users are unfamiliar with. The fact is that Google did not provide a simple way to transfer files onto the Drive. However, we have found a technique to achieve this out of curiosity.

Step 1: Launch your preferred web browser and open Google Drive. If you haven't logged in previously, please enter your login information.

Step 2: Right-click or mouse-over the content of the file you wish to copy.

Step 3 – You will see Make a copy and choose it.

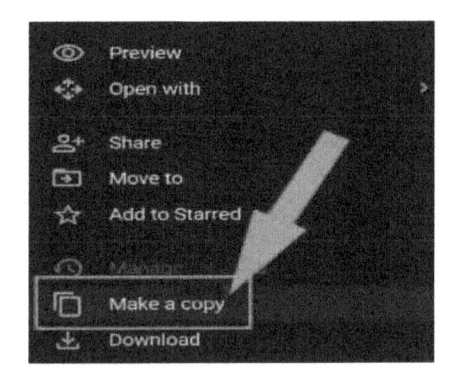

Step 4: Google starts to duplicate every file you've chosen and leaves it in the current folder. Additionally, it prefixes the names of each item with "Copy of."

Step 5 – Right-click on them and, if you'd like, choose to move them to a better place."

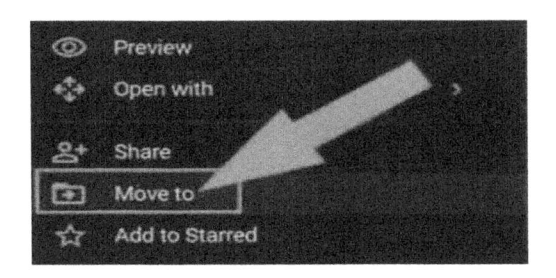

Step 6 – Click on "Move to." This will lead you to choose the new location of the copies.

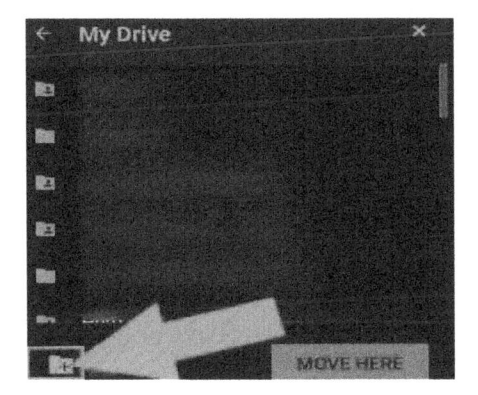

Step 7 – Click "Move Here" so that all your copies move to a new folder.

How To Use Google Drive Offline Mode

If you don't have an internet connection, you can still access your Google Drive offline on your PC, Mac, or mobile device. When you edit your Google Docs, Google Sheets, and Google Slides offline, the updates are applied automatically the next time your device syncs with the internet.

An internet connection and Chrome must not be in incognito mode to set up Google Drive for offline usage. On a Windows-based computer, follow these steps to enable Google Drive offline access:

Step 1: Open the Google Chrome browser.

Step 2: Get the Google Docs offline Chrome extension from the Chrome Web Store and install it.

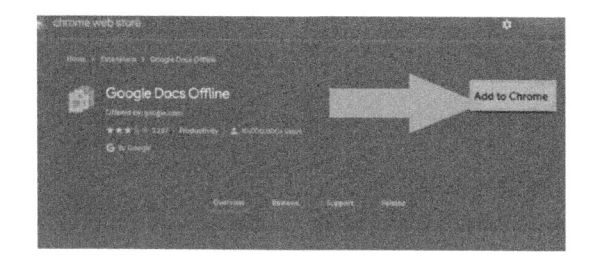

Step 3: If you haven't already, sign into your Google account.

Step 4: Choose Settings (gear symbol) in the top-right corner of your My Drive page.

Step 5: Check the option next to Sync Google Docs, Sheets, Slides & Drawings files to this computer so that you can edit offline after choosing General from the left pane.

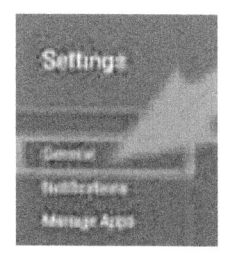

Step 6: Select Done.

Note: If you are using the Chrome web browser, you may now continue working on Google Docs, Google Sheets, or Google Slides files even when you are not connected to the internet. This new feature is only available for those who have upgraded to the latest version of Chrome. The online version will be brought up to date the next time that you connect to the internet, and any changes that you make will be saved in a local cache on your device.

Step 7: Download and set up the free personal edition of Backup and Sync for Google Drive.

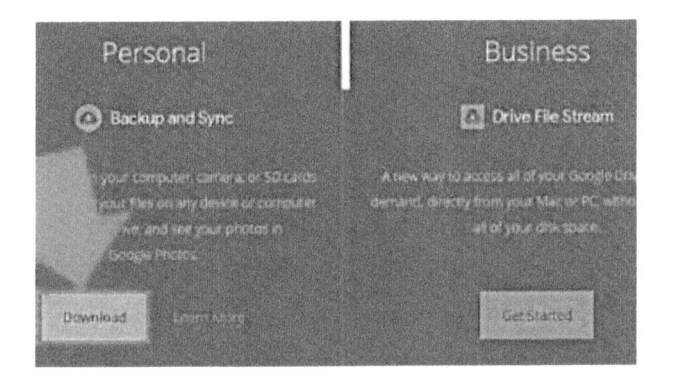

Step 8: Launch Backup and Sync, and after that, login into your Google Account.

Note: You may now instantly save files from your PC to Google Drive if you want to. Deselect the boxes next to each folder if you don't want to do that, then click Next.

Step 9: Select the box beside Sync My Drive to this computer, then select Start.

Your Google Drive files will be downloaded to a folder called Google Drive after a short while, and any further files you upload to Google Drive in the future will also be downloaded automatically to your computer.

One Drive and Google Drive

If you're looking for cloud storage services to manage your company's data conveniently and affordably, then you're likely looking at these two great options: OneDrive and Google Drive. When comparing them head to head, there isn't one that is glaringly better than the other. Rather, it depends upon your specific company's needs.

Microsoft OneDrive is a file hosting and synchronization service provided by Microsoft. It gives the convenience to users for storing files, personal data, and sharing files. It offers 5 GB of free storage space. It was launched by Microsoft in 2007. It is commonly known as OneDrive. It is mostly used by professional workers to store data related to work which might need more security.

Google Drive is a file storage and synchronization service provided by Google. It allows the users to store the files and personal data and to share the files. It offers 15 GB of free storage space. It was launched by Google in 2012. It is used by almost every person and is somehow related to the internet. Everyone uses this to store some professional and personal data.

If your company is looking to stick only to using cloud-based storage, then Google Drive is what you want to choose. However, if your company is looking to use cloud-based storage that also integrates with Windows and Microsoft 365, then OneDrive is the right option.

CHAPTER 3

Google Docs
What Are Google Docs?

Google's browser-based word processor is called Google Docs. Online document creation, editing, and sharing are all accessible from any device with an internet connection. Even iOS and Android mobile apps are available.

Google Docs stands out from its most significant desktop competitor, Microsoft Word, by virtue of its capacity for collaborative writing. Google Docs was one of the first word processors to provide collaborative online document editing when it was first released.

Google has made it very easy to work together in real-time on documents that are being seen in a browser window and to share these documents across several devices. Even if they do not have a Google account, your co-workers will still be able to see and make changes to any Google documents that you share with them.

Additionally, Google Docs add-ons enable you to increase functionality and include omitted capabilities.

The Benefits of Google Docs
1. It works well with Microsoft Word

With the help of this useful Chrome extension, you can quickly access and edit Microsoft Word documents right in Google Docs. Additionally, you may download your Google doc into a Word document (.docx) and vice versa without worrying about formatting changes. Here is information on converting Microsoft Office files to Google Docs.

2. Increase performance using Google Chrome extensions

Google Chrome extensions that you download from the Chrome Web Store may also provide Google Docs additional functionality. By doing so, you'll be able to customize the user experience and give your document new features and functionality.

3. Collaboration is simple.

Teams may easily view and update the same document simultaneously using Google Docs, eliminating any doubt as to which file has the most recent version. Even without a Google account, collaborators may see and modify shared Google documents.

4. Use any device to access your work

You don't have to worry about sending your work to yourself and finding it later using Google Docs since everything is kept in the cloud. You can view your document at any time from any device by logging into your Google account.

5. Automated backup

You never have to worry about files disappearing again since all changes are automatically synchronized across devices and saved as you type. To review previous changes to your document and who made them, you may also check its "**revision history**."

How To Access the Google Docs

You can access your Google documents from any computer, anywhere in the world.

To view a list of documents you own or have access to, or to create a document:

1. Visit Google Drive at https://drive.google.com. Or visit from another Google Apps product.

2. When you're using a Google Apps product like Gmail or Calendar, you'll see other Apps products listed across the top of the page. Click Drive to get started!

3. If you have the new Google One Bar, click at the top of the page and select Drive.

Google Docs User Interface

The Google Drive user interface (UI) is the screen you see when you visit the main Google Drive page with your web browser (located at https://drive.google.com). It's made up of seven main sections and looks something like the following screenshot:

Here is an overview of each section, corresponding to the preceding numbered screenshot.

1 – Files list

Your papers and other files will be shown in the main list, which is referred to as the Files list. It is in most respects comparable to the manner in which files are shown on your personal computer, with the exception that with Google Drive, your files are stored on the cloud.

2 – Toolbars

The toolbars give you quick, one-click access to several important features, with additional actions you can take appearing under the More button. The following toolbar appears when you have selected a document:

3 – Context menu

The Context menu appears when you use the mouse to right-click on a file in the Files list. The menu also appears when you click the More button on the toolbar.

4 – Navigation panel

The Navigation panel appears on the left-hand side of the screen and serves two main purposes. First, under My Drive, your system of folders will appear. This is the folder hierarchy or tree that you may have created (or not—the choice is yours!). Think of it as a filing system that you use to keep your files organized.

Secondly, the Navigation panel lets you quickly change the "views" of your files. For example, you can click on Starred and only those items that you have starred will appear in the Files list.

5 – Preview panel

The Preview panel appears on the right-hand side of the screen and shows you additional details about a selected file. Note that the Preview panel is not shown by default. To show it, first select a file, and then click on the Details icon in the toolbar.

6 – Search bar

The search bar appears at the top of the screen in Google Drive.

7 – Create and upload buttons

The CREATE and upload buttons appear on the left-hand side just above the Navigation panel and are the starting point for creating new documents and files in Google Drive.

Clicking on the CREATE button will display a menu that allows you to choose the type of file you would like to create. To the right-hand side of the CREATE button is the upload button, which you use to upload files from your computer's hard drive directly into Google Drive. The following section shows you how to use these buttons to create new files in Google Drive.

Create Folders on Google Docs

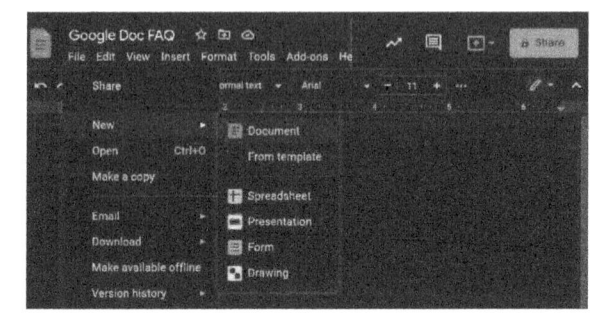

- On your computer, go to drive.google.com.
- On the left, click New. Folder.
- Enter a name for the folder.
- Click Create.

Share Documents on Google Docs

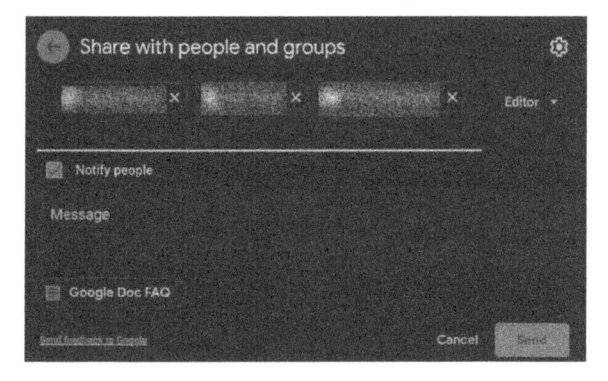

Everyone may access the files and folders that you keep in Google Drive as long as you give them the appropriate permissions. When you share a file from Google Drive, you have the option of controlling whether the recipients may read, modify, or comment on the file.

- Visit Google Drive, Docs, Sheets, or Slides on a computer to create a document.
- Choose the file that you want to share by clicking it.
- Just hit the Share button.

Print Documents from Google Docs

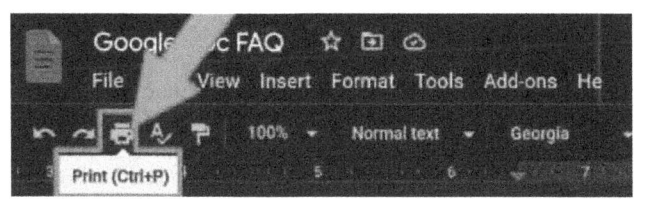

1. Download the Google Docs app on your Android device and open the document you want to print.

2. In the upper-right-hand corner of the Doc, touch the symbol that looks like three vertical dots. This will bring up the **More** menu.

3. From the menu that appears, choose Share & export, then hit the Print button.

4. Locate and choose a printer that is close by.

5. After you have picked your printer and the print options, tap the Print button.

Comparing Google Docs and Microsoft Word

In the business sector during the last several decades, Microsoft Word has been considered the industry standard for word processors everywhere else in the globe. That is now beginning to change, and it seems that one of Google's productivity applications is destined to become the new leader in this space. The Google Docs solution offered by the firm (or, to be more exact, the integrated word processor) is cross-platform and interoperable, syncs automatically, is readily shared, and, probably most importantly, is free.

Functions and features of Microsoft Word

Microsoft Word is a word processing program developed by Microsoft that facilitates the creation of documents by its users. The most recent versions of Microsoft Office come along with pre-made templates that users may apply to documents like resumes. The four most important features of Microsoft Word are as follows.

You must install Microsoft Word on the computer using the Windows operating system. The software is compatible with an overwhelming majority of operating systems, whether desktop or mobile, across a wide range of devices.

Arguably, Word's seamless integration is one of the primary characteristics that give it a greater cutting edge than its competitors. It is possible to use it in conjunction with other applications, such as Microsoft Excel, to do things that were previously challenging, such as importing charts and graphs from Excel to a document created in Word and vice versa.

As was noted previously, Microsoft Word comes with a large selection of pre-designed templates that may be used to rapidly produce professional-looking documents such as resumes. To personalize the document and make it your own, all you need to do is rearrange the positions of the photos, the text, and any other components. In a nutshell, the templates are completely modifiable and have an intuitive interface.

After being familiar with the fundamentals of Microsoft Word, let's move on to Google Docs.

Google Docs Functions and Features

Google Docs is a user-friendly online word processor that was designed to assist users in the creation of word documents across a variety of browsers. It is accessible to everyone who uses Gmail as their primary email service.

Since Google Docs is web-based, there is no need to install it on your computer or mobile device to use it. Making and signing into a Gmail account is all that is required of you at this point. When you hover your cursor over the profile photo associated with your Gmail account, the Docs section of the Google Apps menu will become visible.

Collaborating on a project while working remotely is possible for groups of people who have access to a shared Google Doc and editing permissions. Users of Google Docs have an easier time providing comments or making evaluations, particularly while working asynchronously, because of the platform's intuitive interface.

The fact that Google Docs is entirely free to use is one of its most appealing features. However, over time the amount of space available in your Google Drive will decrease, forcing you to pay for extra storage space as it becomes necessary.

CHAPTER 4

Google Sheets

What Is Google Sheet?

Users are able to create, edit, and alter spreadsheets as well as share data online in real-time while using Google Sheets, a web-based tool that was developed by Google.

The tool offered by Google includes functions often found in spreadsheets, such as the capacity to add, remove, and sort rows and columns. But unlike other spreadsheet tools, Google Sheets allows many users located in different parts of the world to work together simultaneously on a spreadsheet and communicate with one another using an instant messaging program that is incorporated right into the software.

Users can easily upload spreadsheets from either their PCs or mobile devices. Every update that is made is immediately saved by the program, and users can see the changes that have been made by other users as they occur.

The free online application known as Google Sheets is one of the products that are included with the Google Docs Editors package. Google Docs, Google Slides, Google Drawings, Google Forms, Google Sites, and Google Keep are all included with this package from Google.

Spreadsheet collaboration across many geographic areas is often accomplished with the help of Google Sheets. In Google Sheets, many users may make modifications to a document at the same time, and the changes made by each user are logged separately.

Users can create, modify, and format spreadsheets online with the help of the Google Sheets online spreadsheet program. These spreadsheets may then be used to organize and analyse information.

There might be anything from one to several sheets included in a Google spreadsheet. When dealing with a substantial quantity of data, you may find it useful to divide your spreadsheet into numerous sheets to better organize the data and make it simpler to locate certain pieces of information.

How To Access Google Sheet

You can open Sheets in any of the following ways:

- Go to sheets.google.com in any web browser.
- Click New Google Sheets in Google Drive to start from scratch or with a template.
- Click the App Launcher Sheets link in the top-right corner of the majority of Google sites.
- Install and launch the Android app on your Android smartphone.
- Install and launch the iOS software on Apple iOS devices.

Google Sheet User Interface

A Google Sheets GUI can help turn your spreadsheets into real apps.

For businesses, there are several helpful free web tools. And among them, Google Sheets is unquestionably the finest. It enables you to combine the power of scripts, databases, and spreadsheets all at once.

But ultimately, it's still just a spreadsheet tool.

You are therefore constrained to using the grid layout and unfiltered data input. The improper format for data might be added by users. Editing files with several users may get complex. User access control, sophisticated filtering, and search options are absent.

Google Sheets is a versatile data source that may be used with a Graphical User Interface (GUI). It has possibilities for data manipulation, data collection from other websites, and even Apps Script custom function execution.

Users engage with your app simultaneously by utilizing the Google Sheets GUI. As a result, you may manage data input, design unique layouts, include charts and analytics, and establish various user levels.

You may thereby benefit from the best of both worlds. a versatile data source and strong user-facing software.

How To Create Google Sheet

To create a new sheet:

In our example, the sheets of our service log are organized by month. We'll create a new sheet in the log so data can be entered in the new month.

1. Click the Add Sheet command in the sheets toolbar.

2. A new sheet will appear in the sheets toolbar.

Note: Alternatively, you can create an additional sheet by clicking Insert and selecting New sheet from the drop-down menu.

Importing Data into Google Sheets

If there's a file on your computer that you'd like to add to a spreadsheet in Google Sheets, you can. Google Sheets can import several different file types:

- Microsoft Excel (.xls, .xlsx, .xlxm, .xltx, .xltm)
- OpenOffice/LibreOffice (.ods)
- Comma Separated Variable (.csv)
- Tab Separated Variable (.tsv)
- Text files (.txt)
- MapInfo (.tab)

Step 1: Open the document you'd like to import data to, then click File > Import.

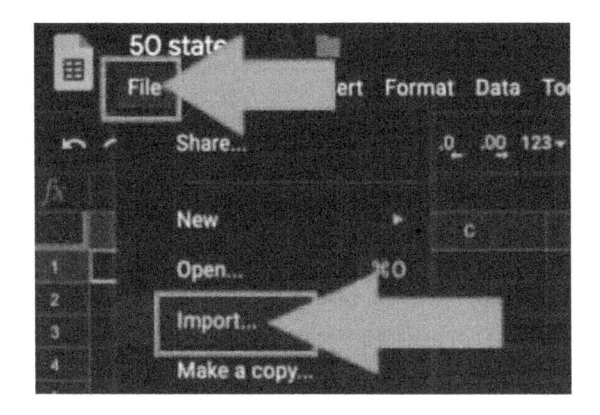

Step 2: From here you can browse files on Google Drive, or you can click Upload to add a file from your computer.

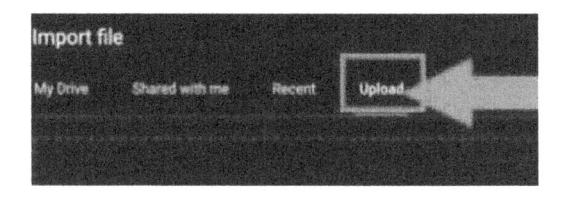

Step 3: You'll have a few options.

73

Step 4: Pick what works best for you and the Imported data will show up.

Formatting Files on Google Sheet

1. Open a spreadsheet in the Google Sheets app.

2. Tap a cell, then drag the blue markers across the nearby cells you want to select.

3. Tap Format.

4. In the "Text" tab, choose an option to format your text.

    - Bold

    - Italic

    - Underline

    - Strikethrough

    - Left text-align

    - Centre text-align

- Right text-align
- Top align (vertical)
- Middle align (vertical)
- Bottom align (vertical)
- Text size, color, and style
- Text Rotation

5. In the "Cell" tab, choose an option to format your cell.

- Cell fill color
- Alternating colors
- Borders
- Cell border
- Border style
- Border color
- Wrap text
- Merge cells

6. Tap the sheet to save your changes.

How To Share Files on Google Sheet

Add the email addresses of your invitees, provide a remark, and then send the invitation to share a Google Sheets file. You may choose whether recipients are just allowed to see, comment on, or change your spreadsheet.

1. Open the spreadsheet you wish to share by creating it or by opening it in Google Sheets.
2. Click Share in the top-right corner of the screen.

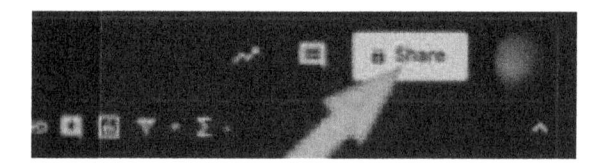

3. Enter the email addresses of the individuals you wish to invite to see, comment on, or modify your Google Sheets file in the Share With People and Groups dialog box.

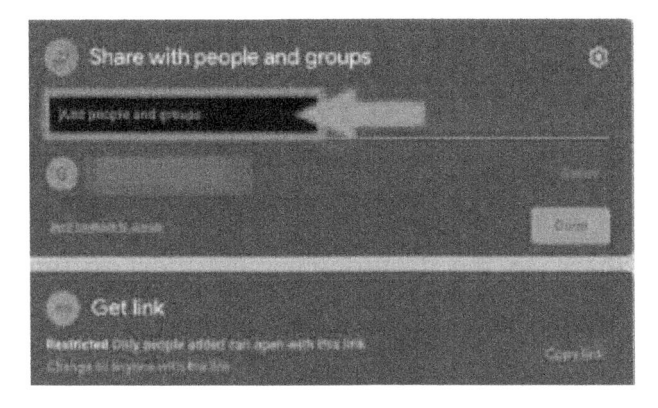

4. Next to the email address field, select the down-arrow and choose one of the three options: Editor, Viewer, or Commenter.

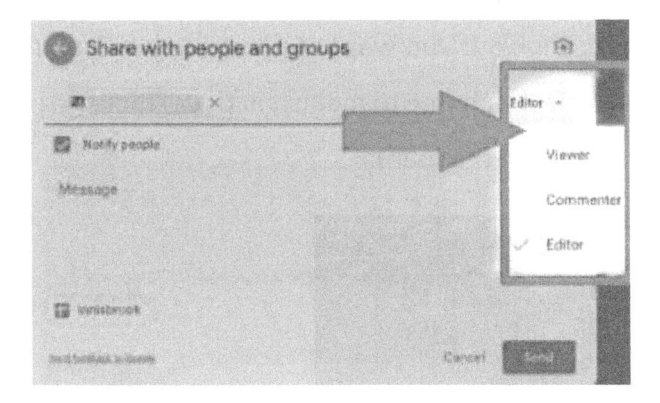

5. Add a note to accompany the invitation, then select Send.

6. As an alternative, open your Google Sheets document, choose Share, and then click Copy

77

Link in the Get link box. The link is copied to your clipboard so you can send it to recipients by pasting it into an email message.

7. To stop sharing a Google Sheets file, select Share. In the drop-down menu next to the collaborator's name, select Remove.

How To Print on Google Sheet

Visit Google Sheets, sign in if necessary, and open the workbook. If you want to print one particular sheet, select that one to make it active. Then, go to File > Print in the menu.

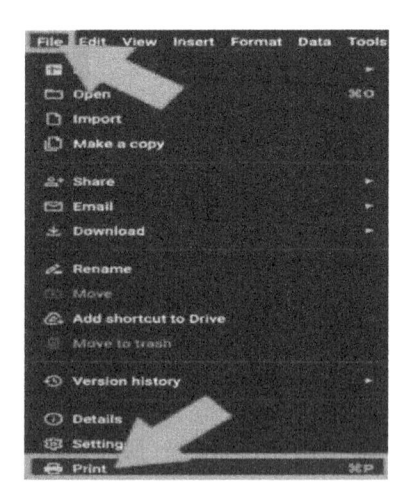

You should see your selected sheet and on the right side under Print, you'll see Current Sheet. You can then adjust the print settings we'll explain in detail below.

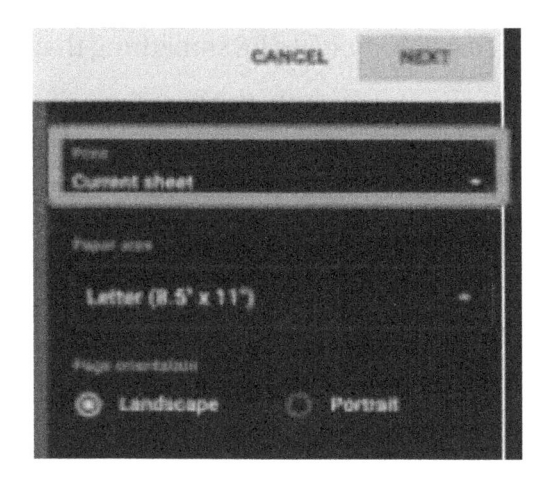

Notice you can also choose to print Selected Cells.

Basic Formulas on Google Sheet

The capability of Google Sheets to automatically add, subtract, multiply, and divide numerical information is a function that is both handy and helpful in terms of saving time. Formulas, which are mathematical expressions, are used inside

Google Sheets to simplify the process of managing these computations. In this section of the course, we will concentrate on formulae that only include a single mathematical operator.

The address of a cell is going to be something that you will be using in the formula the vast majority of the time. Using a cell reference is what you see here. Changing a value in a cell that is referenced by another cell will cause the formula to recalculate automatically if you are using cell references. This is one of the advantages of utilizing cell references. If you include cell references inside your calculations, you may ensure that the numbers that you calculate will be correct.

Google Sheets SUM function

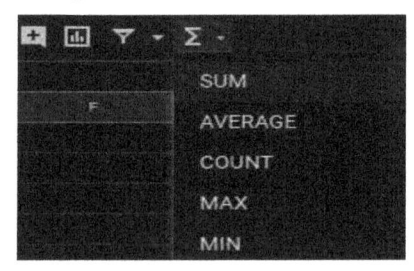

Now, this is one of those Google Sheets functions that you have to learn one way or the other. It adds up several numbers and/or cells and returns their total:

=SUM(value1, [value2, ...])

MAX & MIN functions

The MAX and MIN functions in Google Sheets are used to return the maximum or minimum value in a given range of cells. These functions are helpful when you need to quickly find the highest or lowest value in a dataset. Here's how to use the MAX and MIN functions in Google Sheets.

MAX Function: The MAX function is used to find the largest value in a range of cells. To use the MAX function in Google Sheets, follow these steps:

1. Select the cell where you want to display the result of the MAX function.

2. Type the equal sign (=) to begin the formula.

3. Type MAX followed by an open parenthesis.

4. Select the range of cells that you want to find the maximum value of.

5. Close the parenthesis and press Enter.

For example, if you want to find the maximum value in cells A1:A10, your formula would be =MAX(A1:A10).

MIN Function: The MIN function is used to find the smallest value in a range of cells. To use the MIN function in Google Sheets, follow these steps:

1. Select the cell where you want to display the result of the MIN function.

2. Type the equal sign (=) to begin the formula.

3. Type MIN followed by an open parenthesis.

4. Select the range of cells that you want to find the minimum value of.

5. Close the parenthesis and press **Enter**.

For example, if you want to find the minimum value in cells A1:A10, your formula would be =MIN(A1:A10).

Note that both the MAX and MIN functions can be used with ranges that contain both numeric and non-numeric values. In such cases, the function will ignore non-numeric values and return the maximum or minimum numeric value.

Google Sheets IF function

The IF function in Google Sheets is a conditional function that allows you to test a condition and return one value if the condition is true, and another value if the condition is false. It is a versatile function that can be used in many different scenarios. Here's how to use the IF function in Google Sheets.

Syntax: The syntax for the IF function in Google Sheets is as follows:

=IF(condition, value_if_true, value_if_false)

Where:

- "condition" is the expression or value that you want to test.

- "value_if_true" is the value that will be returned if the condition is true.

- "value_if_false" is the value that will be returned if the condition is false.

Example: Suppose you have a list of numbers in cells A1 to A10, and you want to calculate their sum, but only if they are greater than 5. Here's how you can use the IF function to accomplish this:

1. Select the cell where you want to display the result.

2. Type the equal sign (=) to begin the formula.

3. Type IF followed by an open parenthesis.

4. Enter the condition you want to test, in this case, A1:A10>5.

5. Type a comma (,) to separate the condition from the value_if_true.

6. Enter the formula you want to use if the condition is true, in this case, SUM(A1:A10).

7. Type a comma (,) to separate the value_if_true from the value_if_false.

8. Enter the formula you want to use if the condition is false, in this case, 0.

9. Close the parenthesis and press Enter.

Your final formula should look like this:

=IF(A1:A10>5, SUM(A1:A10), 0)

This formula will test each value in the range A1:A10, and if it is greater than 5, it will add it to the sum. If it is less than or equal to 5, it will be ignored.

COUNT & COUNTA

The Google Sheets functions COUNT and COUNTA may both be used to count the number of data-containing cells in a range of cells.

As contrast to COUNTA, which counts all non-blank cells regardless of whether they include data like text, numeric values, or other sorts of data, COUNT exclusively counts cells that have numeric values.

Here is a quick rundown of each Google Sheets feature and how to utilize it:

Google Sheets' COUNT function can be utilized to determine how many cells in a range contain numerical data. The COUNT function has the following syntax:

=COUNT(range)

The range of cells you wish to count is indicated by the "range" argument. For instance, you might use the formula shown below to determine how many cells in the range A1:A10 have numeric values.

=COUNT(A1:A10)

The COUNTA function in Google Sheets is used to determine how many of a range of cells are not blank. The COUNTA function has the following syntax:

=COUNTA(range)

The range of cells you wish to count is indicated by the "range" argument. For instance, you might use the following formula to count the number of cells in the range A1:A10 that are not blank:

=COUNTA(A1:A10)

Keep in mind that the COUNTA function counts both cells with numeric values and cells with text or other non-numeric values.

Calculating Averages on Google Sheet

Calculating averages on Google Sheets is a straightforward process. Here are the steps to follow:

1. Select the cell where you want to display the average value.

2. Type the equal sign (=) to begin the formula.

3. Type the function name "AVERAGE" in uppercase letters, followed by an open parenthesis "(".

4. Select the range of cells that you want to average. You can either click and drag to select the range or manually type the cell references separated by commas.

5. Close the parenthesis ")" and press enter.

For example, if you want to calculate the average of the values in cells A1 to A10, the formula would be:

=AVERAGE(A1:A10)

Working with Functions and Percentage

You could be interested in obtaining the average of cells that are not next to one another, numbers, or a mix of cells and numbers. In this particular scenario, manually inputting the AVERAGE function is going to provide you with the greatest results. Because of this, you have the option to add whatever it is that you need to the formula.

In Google Sheets, the syntax for the function is written as AVERAGE(value1, value2), where value1 is necessary but value2 is optional.

Choose the cell in which you would want the average to be shown. In this first example, we will calculate the average of two groups of cells that are not contiguous to one another: groups B2 through B12 and E2 through E12. To use this formula, you would insert it into your spreadsheet with your cell references substituting those in the following formula.

=AVERAGE(B2:B12,E2:E12)

If the values that you wish to average do not already exist inside the cells of the spreadsheet, you may easily find their average by entering those numbers into the formula.

=AVERAGE(5,10,15,20,100,120)

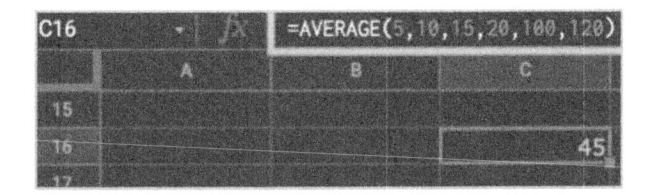

In the formula, you may also mix cell data and numerical values. Using the information below, we will now calculate the average of the numbers 10 and 15, the range of cells B2 through B12, and cell E12.

=AVERAGE(10,15,B2:B12,E12)

The percentage (%) format is often considered to be among the most useful of all number formats. It presents the information in the form of percentages, such as 20% or 55%. This comes in very handy when figuring out things like the amount of sales tax that has to be paid or a tip. After you write a number, the percentage number format will be immediately applied to that cell the moment you type a percent sign (%) after the number.

You may recall from your time spent studying mathematics that a percentage may also be represented as a decimal. Therefore, 15% is equal to 0.15, 7.5% is equal to 0.075, 20% is equal to 0.20, 55% is equal to 0.55, and so on.

The formatting of percentages may be quite helpful in a variety of contexts. For instance, have a look at the photos below to see how the structure of the sales tax rate is presented differently in each spreadsheet (5, 5%, and 0.05):

It is clear that the calculation in the spreadsheet on the left did not provide the expected results. Due to the fact that our spreadsheet does not include the percentage number format, it is under the impression that the required operation is to multiply $22.50 by 5, rather than 5%. The spreadsheet on the right may be utilized without the % formatting, but the spreadsheet in the middle is much simpler to understand.

How to Create Charts and Graphs in Google Sheet

Google Sheets gives you a variety of options for your graph, so if you want to show parts that make up a whole you can go for a pie chart, and if you want to compare statistics, a bar graph will likely make more sense. Here are our step-by-step instructions for making a graph in Google Sheets.

1. Select cells. If you're going to make a bar graph like we are here, including a column of names and values and a title to the values.

2. Click Insert.

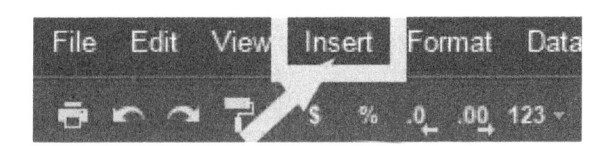

3. Select Chart.

4. Select which kind of chart. Pie charts are best when all of the data adds up to 100 percent, whereas histograms work best for data compared over time.

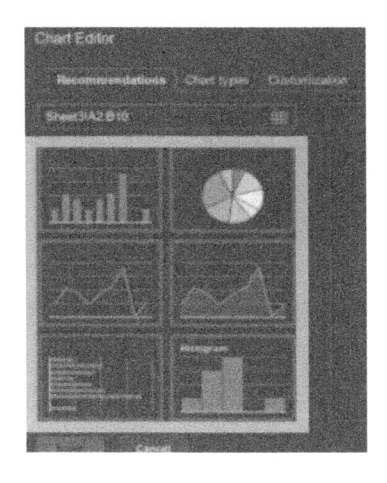

5. Click Chart Types for options including switching what appears in the rows and columns or other kinds of graphs.

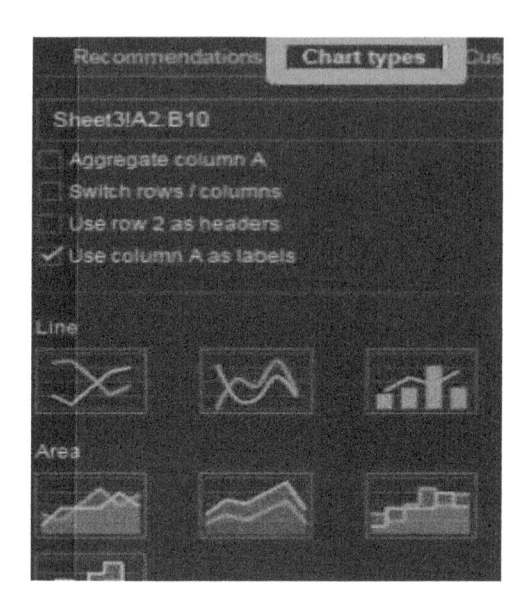

6. Click Customization for additional formatting options.

7. Click Insert.

You've inserted a graph into your spreadsheet.

Excel Vs Google Sheet

If we're talking about cost, Google Sheets don't cost anything. They are at your disposal anytime you want and wherever you want to utilize them.

You will be required to pay a monthly fee of $5 if you decide to sign up for a membership for your company. If you pay for a whole year's worth of services at once, Google will give you a discount. On the other hand, Microsoft Office cannot be obtained without paying for it. You will be required to pay a fee of $8.25 a month for a single user to make use of Microsoft Office 365 (just the online version).

One further benefit of using Google Sheets is how simple it is to work with other people. If you are currently working on a Google Sheet and believe that you may benefit from the assistance of your team in producing something of value, you can invite your team to participate and contribute their insights by asking them to join in. It gives the impression that numerous users may work together on a Google Sheet at the same time. As a direct consequence of this, working together is simplified. On the other hand, Microsoft Excel enables users to monitor changes made in the spreadsheet, but Google Sheets enables users to concurrently make edits to the sheet.

Those who use Macbooks are more likely to choose Google Sheets over Microsoft Excel since the former may be compatible with all programs, while Excel was designed primarily for Windows users and not Mac users.

If you are going to utilize Microsoft Excel, you will need to save the file by hand. On the other hand, if you use Google Sheets, you can focus on producing the sheet and getting the important job done, and the sheet will be stored on your Google Drive without any further action required from you.

Excel and Google Sheets are equally impressive pieces of software in terms of the fundamental capabilities that they provide. Excel is the superior tool for you to use if the nature of your work involves doing complex mathematical calculations. Google Sheets is your best choice if you want to work with other people on your spreadsheet at the same time.

CHAPTER 5

Google Slides

What Is Google Slides?

A presentation graphics application from Google that is part of its Google Docs suite. Google Slides is similar to Microsoft's venerable PowerPoint program, and presentations are created from within the browser.

It includes nearly all the capabilities of a traditional presentation program, such as Microsoft PowerPoint. The cloud storage that Google Slides provides for its customers means that their papers are automatically stored and may be accessed even if the user's local hard disk or solid-state drive ceases to function properly.

How To Access Google Slides

Open the Slides home screen at slides.google.com. In the top left, under "Start a new presentation," click New. This will create and open your new presentation.

Creating a New Presentation

To create a new presentation:

1. Open the Slides home screen at slides.google.com.

2. In the top left, under "**Start a new presentation**," click New Plus. This will create and open your new presentation.

3. You can also create new presentations from the URL https://slides.google.com/create.

How to Add Slides to your Presentation

To add a slide with the same layout as the current slide:

- On your computer, open a presentation in Google Slides.
- In the top left, click New slide.

To add a slide with a different layout:

- On your computer, open a presentation in Google Slides.
- In the top left, click New slide with the layout.
- Choose a slide.

Google Slide User Interface

When you use Google Slides to create a new presentation, the user interface for Google Slides will become visible. The toolbar is shown inside this user interface, in addition to the primary view of your presentation. It gives you the ability to create and alter slides, choose a theme for the presentation, and share it with other people.

A sample of your slides will be shown in the sidebar that is located on the left side of the screen. You have the option of seeing your slides either as a filmstrip or in a grid format at the very bottom of the screen.

You may begin with one of the preset themes that can be seen on the right side. You may concentrate on your design by just clicking the X in the top right corner of the window if you do not need them.

At the top, you will see the file name "**Untitled presentation**". Just clicking on it will allow you to create a name that is pertinent to your document, making it much simpler to locate among the rest of your Google Slides presentations or in Drive.

The Menu Bars

The user interface for Google Slides is based on a typical menu structure and also includes a shortcut toolbar. The commands are organized into categories according to their purposes in the menus. The shortcut toolbar has buttons for some of the most often-used tasks.

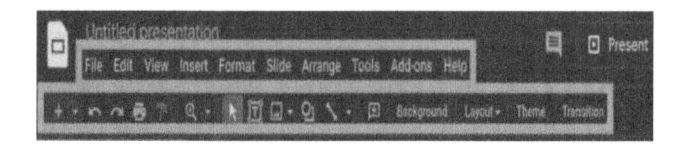

You have the option to reduce the size of the navigation bar, which will make more room available for displaying your slides. You may conceal the menu bar by selecting the option to "**Hide the menus**," after which the only toolbar shown at the top of the window will be the shortcut toolbar. Simply clicking it once more will display the menu bar once again.

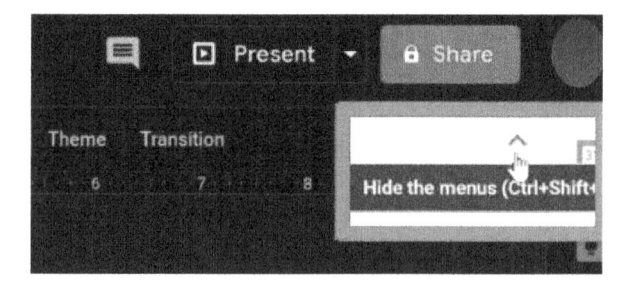

Utilizing the shortcut for Zoom, you can zoom in and out of your presentation. After clicking the Zoom button on the shortcut toolbar, drag the mouse cursor over the slide you want to zoom in on. The cursor will transform into a **+** symbol inside a magnifying glass when you choose this option. You may now use the left mouse button to zoom in, and the right mouse button to zoom out. You can reset your cursor to its usual state by using the Escape key on your keyboard.

If you go to the View drop-down menu and hover your mouse pointer over the Zoom option, you will find options that allow you to select the zoom level more accurately.

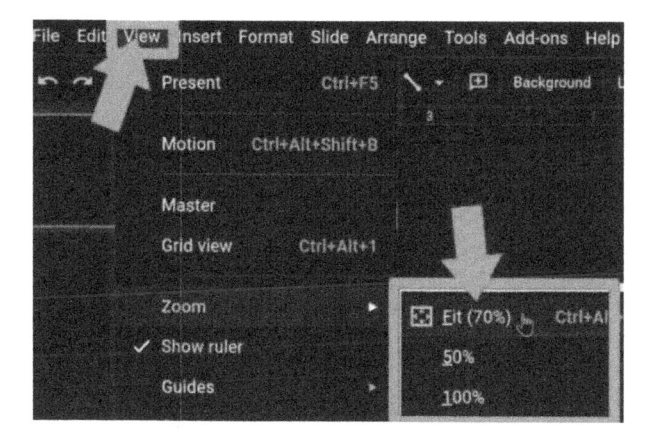

Setting Up your Slide

Go to Google's home page and click on the grid in the upper right-hand corner. From there, click on the Drive icon. You will be redirected to a login page if you are signed out, if not you will be taken to your Drive.

- To create a new file on your Drive, go to the left side of the screen and select the blue button labeled New. Choose "Google Slides" from the available options in the drop-down menu.
- If you are already on the slides page, you may make a new slide by selecting an item from the menu at the top of the page.

Adding More Slides

Step 1: Go to https://drive.google.com/drive/my-drive to access your Google Drive, then choose the presentation to which you want to add a new slide.

Step 2: From the column on the left side of the window, choose the slide to which you want to add the new slide.

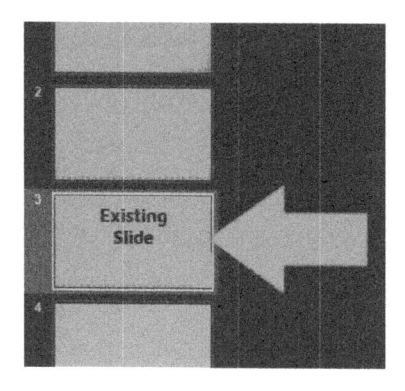

Step 3: Pick the **Insert** tab at the top of the window.

Step 4: Click the **New slide** option at the bottom of the window.

Keep in mind that you can also add a new slide by clicking the **+** button above the column of slides or by typing the keyboard shortcut Ctrl + M. As an alternative, you may choose one of many formats for your new slide by clicking the arrow to the right of that + button.

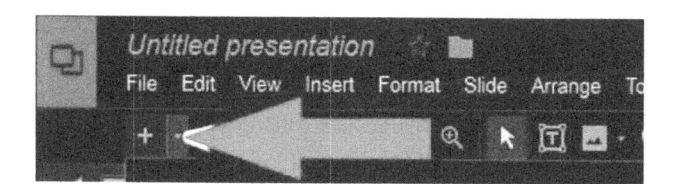

How to Insert Text on Your Slide

1. Launch a Google Slides presentation on your PC.

2. Navigate to the slide where a text box or other item should be added.

3. Press the Insert button up top.

4. After selecting your addition, pick Text box, Image, Shape, or Line.

5. After the item is put on the slide, you may format or organize it in any way you want.

On a touchscreen device like a Pixel Book, double-tap the text box to begin typing to change a presentation.

How to Format Your Slide

- **Change the size of your slides**

Step 1: On your computer, open a presentation in Google Slides.

Step 2: Click File.

To pick a size, click the Down arrow. Standard (4:3) Widescreen (16:9) Widescreen (16:10) Custom: Below "Custom," enter a size and pick a unit of measurement (inches, centimeters, points, or pixels).

Step 3: Click OK.

- **Edit your theme colors**

Step 1: On your computer, open a presentation in Google Slides.

Step 2: At the top, click Slide then Edit theme.

Step 3: At the top, click Colors Color.

Step 4: To the right, under "Theme colors," choose the color you want to edit from the drop-down.

Import Files to Google Slides

1. Open a presentation.

2. Select Import Slides under File.

3. Decide whether to upload a presentation from your computer or choose one from Drive.

4. Click Select.

5. Select the desired presentation slides by clicking on them. To easily pick all slides, use the Select Slides: All option.

6. If you wish to import the slides in their original form, check the Keep original theme box. If you want the slides to match the style of your new presentation, uncheck the option.

7. Select Import Slides

How to Apply Transition and Animation on Google Slides

- To add a transition:

Select the desired slide, then click the Transition command on the toolbar.

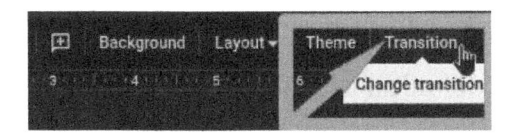

The Motion pane will appear. Underneath Slide Transition, open the drop-down menu; then, select a transition.

The transition will be applied to the current slide. You also can adjust the speed of the transition or apply the same transition to all slides.

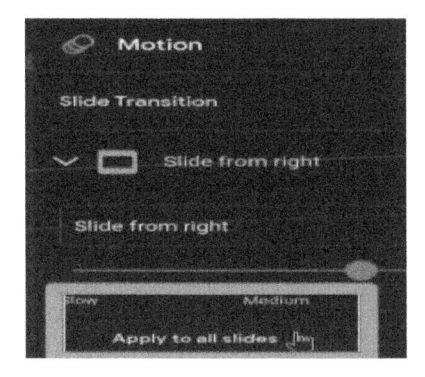

- **To add an animation:**

Right-click the desired object, then select **Animate**.

The Motion pane will appear. Underneath Object Animations, a default animation will be added to the selected object and displayed in the pane.

Open the drop-down menu and select the desired animation.

Note: If the Motion pane is already open and you want to add more animations, you can select an object and click **Add animation**. You can also add multiple animations to one object.

How to Apply Animation in Slides

1. On your computer, open a presentation in Google Slides.

2. Click the text or image you want to animate.

3. Click Insert Animation.

How to Share Presentation on Google Slides

Google Drive makes sharing your files simple. It also allows multiple people to edit the same file, allowing for real-time collaboration.

To share a file with a limited group of people:

Find the file you wish to share, select it, and then click the **Share** button.

There will be a dialog box. Enter the email addresses of the individuals you want to share the file with in the People box. You may provide a note that will be sent to the recipients of the file if you want.

Select Send. It will be shared with others.

To share a link:

1. Find the file you wish to share, then click the Share button when you've made your selection.

2. A new window for the dialog box will open. Just click the Obtain Shareable Link button.

Please take note that a link to the file will be transferred to the clipboard of your web browser. After that, you may distribute the file by pasting the URL into an email message or posting it on the web. After you are done, be sure you click the Done button.

How to Publish your Presentation on Google Slide

1. In Google Drive, open your file.
2. From Docs, Sheets, Slides, select File.
3. Publish to the web.

Note:

- For spreadsheets, select the entire spreadsheet or individual sheets.
- For presentations, choose how quickly to advance the slides.

4. Click Publish.

5. Copy the link and send it to anyone you'd like to share the file with.

Google Slide Vs Microsoft PowerPoint

PowerPoint is better suited for making presentations that are more conventional, while Google Slides is superior when it comes to the ability to create presentations that are interactive and simple to browse.

PowerPoint, on the other hand, may be more suited for face-to-face meetings, but slides may be utilized to produce visually appealing information that is simple to distribute online.

Because there are no templates to work with in Google Slides, its user interface is simpler and more intuitive to use than that of PowerPoint. If you want to alter the font size on a certain slide, all you have to do is click on the icon that represents the font size, and then choose the font size that you would want to use.

The URL to the presentation may be easily sent to other individuals, which enables them to see it without any effort on their part.

You are also able to check at any moment to see who is watching your presentation. You also have the option to save the presentation and return to it at a later time by clicking on the option that says "save as."

Because it includes capabilities such as timeline playback and animated gifs, Google Presentations is the superior option for creating slides with transitions. PowerPoint also has some fantastic transition choices, but the number of those possibilities is far lower than what's available in Google Slides. If you require more than just the most fundamental transitions, then PowerPoint is probably the best option for you to go with.

CHAPTER 6

Google Forms

What Is Google Form?

Google Forms is a piece of software that can be accessed online for free and used to create surveys, quizzes, and other similar applications. It is a component of Google's suite of web-based applications, which also consists of Google Docs, Google Sheets, and Google Slides, amongst others. It is a flexible instrument that may be put to use for a variety of purposes, such as compiling a list of people who have shown interest in attending an event or developing a quick quiz.

To create a Google Form, you'll need a Google account; but, the options for the form may be changed so that it can be completed by anybody, regardless of whether or not they have a Google account.

The Benefit of Using Google Form

Google forms are widely used to create surveys easily and quickly since they allow you to plan events, ask questions to your employees or clients and collect the diverse type of information simply and efficiently.

It is a free online tool that allows you to collect information easily and efficiently.

With Google forms, you can create surveys in a few minutes to ask your clients or collaborators for information about your products or service.

To start using this tool, you only need a Google account, the same one you need to access Gmail, YouTube, or Google Drive.

The interface is very easy to use. Any user with average Internet knowledge can create forms using this tool.

You don't need any specialized software to generate and evaluate surveys using Google

Forms; you can do both straight in the browser of your mobile device or computer. You are provided with quick results as they are received. In addition, you can quickly summarize the findings of the survey by using charts and graphs.

How To Access Google Forms

Step 1: Set up a new form or quiz. Go to forms.google.com.

Step 2: Edit and format a form or quiz. You can add, edit, or format text, images, or videos in a form. ...

Step 3: Send your form for people to fill out. When you are ready, you can send your form to others and collect their responses.

Google Form User Interface

The form interface includes two tabs at the top of your form. Click the appropriate one to edit your form or to view the responses. Question logic: Send the user to a specific section based on their answer to a question. Only available with Multiple choice and Dropdown question types.

It is a fantastic method for designing an online survey or having individuals input data for different reasons. It is also important to note that Google Forms has been partially decoupled from Google Sheets. This means that it is now possible to create a form directly from Google Drive and view the results within Google Forms, rather than having to open up Google Sheets. This is a significant improvement over the previous situation, which required users to open Google Sheets.

How to Create a Google Form

Google Forms differentiates itself from similar online software through its library of customization options. When creating your new form, you'll have the ability to select from a series of templates or design your very own. If you choose to make a new template, consider adding your logo and photos, and watch Google generate a custom color set to match.

1. Open Google Forms: Go to the Google Forms homepage (https://docs.google.com/forms) and sign in to your Google account.

2. Start a new form: Click on the "+" sign or the "Blank" button to start a new form.

3. Create a form title: Type in a title for your form in the "Untitled form" field.

4. Add questions: Click on the "+ Add question" button to start adding questions to your form. You can choose from a variety of question types, such as multiple choice, short answer, paragraph, etc.

5. Customize your questions: After selecting a question type, enter the question text and any

other required information such as answer choices, options, or guidelines.

6. Add additional sections: You can add additional sections by clicking on the "Add section" button to organize your form and group related questions together.

7. Configure form settings: Click on the "Settings" gear icon at the top right corner of the screen to configure various settings such as form responses, presentation options, and notifications.

8. Preview and test the form: Click on the "Preview" button to view and test your form before sharing it.

9. Share the form: Once your form is ready, you can share it with others by clicking on the "Send" button at the top right corner of the screen. You can share the form via email, social media, or embed it on a website.

10. View responses: After your form is shared, you can view responses by clicking on the "Responses" tab at the top of the screen. You can also choose to export the responses to a Google Sheet for further analysis.

Question Types

Google Forms contain lots of different types of questions which should match most of your needs. They include:

Short answer

When you want the form-filler to write a short answer. They can write a longer answer, but the box is small so they can only see a few words.

Paragraph

When you want the form-filler to write a longer answer. The box is bigger than a Short Answer so they can see what they've written.

Checkboxes

Similar to multiple-choice questions but here form-fillers can select more than one option.

Drop-down

The same as multiple-choice questions, except that the form-filler doesn't see the options until they click on the drop-down menu.

Multiple-choice grid

The rows are the different questions or areas, and the columns are usually the opinions, but you could set it up for other uses too. It's like having lots of multiple-choice questions joined together.

Importing a Question

Visit Google Forms, sign in, and open the form you want to pull questions into.

Select the question where you want to insert an imported question below. Then, click the Import Questions icon in the toolbar to the right.

You also have the option of moving the questions you are importing to the very top of your form, rather of placing them underneath a particular question. To do this, you must refrain from selecting an existing question before moving on. Merely import the questions by making use of the toolbar, and they will be displayed at the very top. After then, reorder them at a later time.

Find the form that contains the questions you wish to utilize and go to it. If you have a lot of forms, you can find the one you need quickly by using the Search box that is located at the top or the **Sort** button that is located on the right.

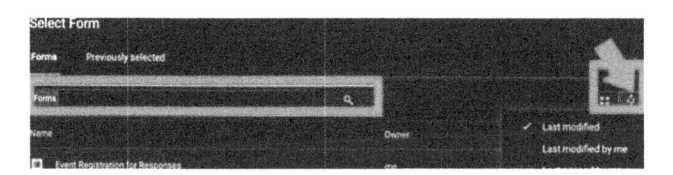

Choose the form and click "**Select**."

The questions from the form you select will display in the sidebar on the right. If you realize you have the wrong form, click "**Change Form**" and find the correct one.

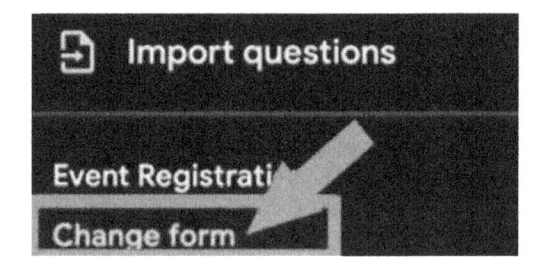

You can then pick **Select All** to use all questions or just check the boxes for the questions you want. When you finish, click "**Import Questions**."

If you want to reuse additional questions from other forms, you can do this as well. Just follow the same steps to locate and select the form and choose the questions. This will give you a form that's ready to use in no time!

Viewing Responses

1. Open a form in Google Forms.

2. At the top of the form, click Responses.

3. Click Summary.

Sending And Sharing Google Forms

Simply click the Send button located in the upper right corner of the page to send the form to others by email or social networks, copy a link to the form, or get an embed code to include it on your website.

With the link, you can either copy a full-length link or get a shortened goo.gl/forms/ link to share more easily on social networks. The embed option includes width and height options to fit the form within your site's design.

Sharing the form via email includes an extra option: including the form in the email. This copies your actual form options into the email, and if your recipient uses Gmail, they can fill out the form inside their Gmail inbox, click Submit, and send in their answer without ever seeing your real form.

One of Google Forms' best features is that you can share the core form with others to let them help you build and edit the form. The same sharing features you'd expect in Google Docs and Sheets are included with Forms.

Just open the Forms menu and select Add Collaborators, then enter individual collaborators' email addresses. Or click Change... to make the form public to the web or just inside your organization.

Using a Template

Choose one of the featured templates from the home screen for Docs, Sheets, Slides, Forms, Sites. This may be done at the top of the screen. To see further templates, click on the Gallery of Templates button.

Note: If you can't seem to locate the Template gallery, you may toggle its visibility by going to Display or hide the Template gallery.

If you already have a file open in one of the Docs editors, select the File menu item, and then click the and then and then button.

From the available templates, choose the one that best fits your needs.

To use a pre-existing template, go to Drive, select the New button, then next to Google Docs, Sheets, Slides, or Sites, click the Right arrow next to "From a template."

CHAPTER 7

GOOGLE KEEP

What Is Google Keep?

Google Keep is Google's version of a note-taking app — but there's more to it than basic checklists or quick thoughts taken down in a moment of inspiration.

For one thing, since it's made by Google, it automatically syncs to Google Drive, so you can access it from any device where you use your Google account, whether it be a computer, your phone, or your tablet. That way, you don't have to go digging around your various accounts or devices to find the right note.

Benefits of Using Google Keep

Google Keep is a note-taking service developed by Google to help you quickly capture whatever is on your mind.

- We can Capture, edit, share, and collaborate on the notes using any device, from anywhere.
- We can Arrange the notes with labels and colors.
- We can Add notes, lists, photos, and audio to Keep.
- Just Set and forget. We will be reminded about a note at the right time at the right place.
- We can Record a voice memo and have it automatically transcribed.
- We can Grab the text from an image and quickly find that note again just through a simple search.

Access Google Keep

To get started with Google Keep, you'll need to choose a platform. The Keep Android app is available in the Google Play Store for phones and smartwatches, and iPhone and iPad users will find the Keep app in the App Store. It also works in most web browsers through the desktop app, and there's a Google Keep web clipper extension in the Chrome Web Store.

To access Google Keep, you can use the mobile app (available on both Android and iOS devices), or go to keep.google.com. (There's also a Chrome browser extension you can download for it.)

Google Keep Interface

Google Keep interface for Keep almost resembles a wall of sticky notes, allowing you to rearrange them as desired.

The interface allows for a single-column view or a multi-column view. Notes can be color-coded and labels can be applied to notes to categorize them. Later updates have added functionality to pin notes and to collaborate on notes with other Keep users in real-time.

How to Create and Edit Notes on Google Keep

To create a note

1. On your Android phone or tablet, open the Google Keep app.

2. Tap Create Add.

3. Add a note and title.

4. When you're done, tap Back.

To Edit a note

1. On your Android phone or tablet, open the Google Keep app.

2. Tap the note you want to edit.

3. Make changes to a note.

4. To undo an action, tap Undo.

5. To redo an action, tap Redo.

6. When you're done, tap Back.

Making a List

1. On your Android phone or tablet, open the Google Keep app Google Keep.

2. Next to "Take a note," tap New list.

3. Add a title and items to your list.

4. When you're done, tap Back

To Make a Sketch

1. On your computer, go to Google Keep.

2. At the top, click New note with drawing .

3. To start drawing, click and drag in the drawing area.

4. To save the drawing, click Back.

5. In the bottom right, click Done.

Note:

- To edit your drawing, open the note and click the drawing.

- To make the drawing area bigger, draw at the bottom of the screen and scroll up.

Making a New Note with an Image

Follow these steps to create a new image note on Google Keep using your computer.

Step 1: First of all, you have to go to keep.google.com present on your computer.

Step 2: Near the top of the page, you have to click the New note with the image.

Step 3: Here, you need to pick a photo from your computer's library.

Step 4: Now, you can also enter a title and text for your note.

Step 5: At last, when you're finished, click Done or outside the note.

How to Organize Your Different Notes

With Google Keep's built-in features, you can organize your notes by color-coding, labeling, and pinning them. To add more details, you can also insert images and links. Each note can be customized and categorized the way you want.

Add Labels

Because it does not allow folders and subfolders, Google Keep does not have a hierarchical structure. On the other hand, you can use labels to organize your notes. You may add several labels to a note. Labels function similarly to tags in that they assist in determining the category of the note. Labels for categories such as "work," "personal," "travel," and so on might be included in your notes. When you need to discover the notes that are linked to work in the future, all you need to do is click on the label that says "work."

The following actions need to be taken to add labels to a note:

1. Open Google Keep: Go to the Google Keep homepage (https://keep.google.com/) and sign in to your Google account.

2. Create a new note: Click on the "**Take a note**" field or the "**New note**" button to create a new note.

3. **Add labels to the note**: Once you have created the note, click on the three vertical dots (more actions) icon at the bottom right corner of the note. Then select "Add label" from the drop-down menu.

4. Create a new label or select an existing one: You can either create a new label by typing in a name for it, or select an existing label from the list of suggested labels.

5. Apply the label: Once you have selected or created the label, click on the "Done" button to apply the label to the note.

6. View labeled notes: To view all notes with a particular label, click on the label name in the left-hand menu. You can also search for notes with a specific label by typing the label name in the search bar.

Pin Notes

You can accomplish this by pinning them to the top of the page if you have any essential notes that you want to make sure are constantly accessible there. The pinned notes will continue to appear on top of existing notes even when you add new ones, much like the pin function seen in other applications.

Open a note inside the Google Keep mobile app, and then hit the pin symbol that is located at the very top of the message.

On the website, hover over the note and click on the pin icon.

To-Do Lists

To-do lists have been a component of Google Keep for quite some time, even though Google only recently introduced a standalone tool for managing to-dos called Google Tasks. You can make a new list of things to do by pressing the icon labeled "**New list**." Tap the checkbox to indicate that the task has been finished once you have created it.

You can also convert an existing note into a to-do list. To do it on the website, tap the three-dot icon and select **Show checkboxes**.

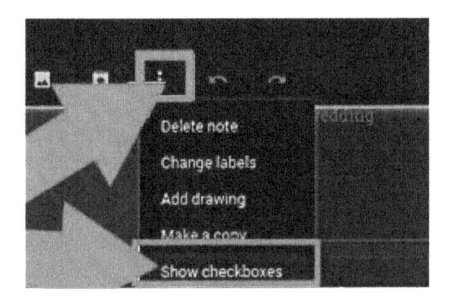

On mobile apps, tap the plus icon at the bottom-left corner and hit **Tick boxes**.

Mark by Color

Another way to find notes easily is by using the color scheme. By default, all the notes are white, but Google Keep lets you change their color for easier identification. For instance, you can keep your lists in yellow and all personal notes in green.

To change the note color on the mobile apps, tap the three-dot menu in an individual note and select one from the available colors.

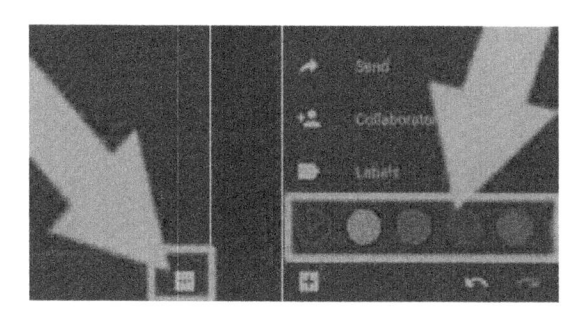

On the website, open the note and click on the color-palette icon. Then select the color.

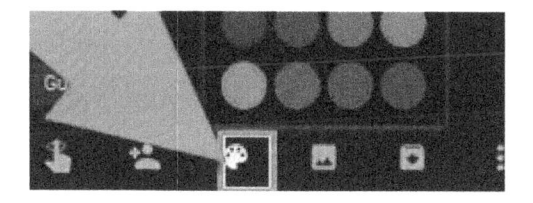

How to Share Notes and Collaborate on Google Keep

1. On your Android phone or tablet, open the Google Keep app.

2. Tap the note you want to share.

3. Tap **Action**.

4. Tap **Collaborator**.

5. Enter a name, email address, or Google Group.

6. Choose a name or email address. To remove someone from a note, tap Remove.

7. In the top right, tap Save.

Archives and Reminder

Archive is a smart way to clean up the home screen of the Google Keep app. It hides your notes from the main view. Consider it as a special folder in Google Keep where you can hide your notes. When a note is archived, it disappears from the main screen of the Google Keep app and goes into the Archive section.

To do this:

Launch the Google Keep app on your mobile. Tap on the note that you want to archive. Tap on the Archive icon at the top-right corner.

Alternatively, touch and hold the note on the main screen of the Google Keep app. When the note is selected, tap on the three-dot icon at the top and choose **Archive**.

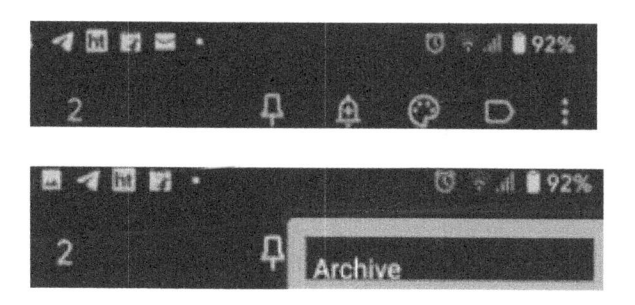

- Using reminders on your Google keep

Step 1: On your Android phone or tablet, open the Keep app.

Step 2: Tap a note.

Step 3: In the top right, tap Remind me.

You can set reminders to go off at a certain time or place:

- Time reminder: Tap one of the default times or tap Pick a date & time. You can also set the reminder to repeat.
- Location reminder: Tap Place. Then enter the name or address and tap Save. You'll need to let Keep access your location.

Step 4: Your note's reminder appears below the note text next to any labels.

Step 5: To close your note, tap Back.

Step 6: To change or delete your reminder, tap the reminder time or place it at the bottom of the note.

How to Export your Google Keep Note

Google Keep has a 19,999 characters limit per note, so once a note gets too long, you'll have to export it to Google Docs to keep the creative flow going.

To export to Google Docs, you have to do it manually, one note at a time, but it's more likely you'll be doing it as a note runs out of room or as you transition from planning to drafting for things like term papers and reports.

Open Google Keep on your phone or in a computer browser.

1. Tap the note you want to export.

2. Tap the three-dot menu icon at the bottom of the note

3. Tap Send (app only).

4. Tap **Copy to Google Docs**.

Google Keep Chrome Extension

Installing the extension for your Chrome browser is quite simple if you follow these steps:

1. Make sure you log in to your Google account on the Chrome browser.

2. Visit the Google Keep extension on the Chrome Web Store.

3. Select the Add to Chrome button.

4. Click Add extension on the pop-up that follows.

5. Another pop-up will let you know that the extension has been added.

6. Now click on the Extensions icon in the top-left corner of Chrome.

7. Click on the Pin beside Keep to make it visible near the address bar.

How to Disable Chrome Extensions

Chrome Extensions are programs that improve your browsing experience by allowing you to optimize Google Chrome for your individual needs. They may be anything, from ad blockers to mail checks to translation tools to add-ons for antivirus software. On the other hand, if you try to utilize them, and every time you do, they either stop functioning or crash, it's time to deactivate them.

Here's how to disable your Chrome extensions:

1. Open the Chrome browser, click the three-dot menu icon in the upper right corner.

2. Click on More tools >Extensions.

3. Simply click the toggle button of the extension you want to disable.

Disabling extensions is an effective way to improve your browser's speed, especially if you notice that webpages are loading slowly or that you can't open videos on YouTube.

CHAPTER 8

Google Photos

What Are Google Photos?

Google Photos is one of the world's most popular photo storage and sharing services. People often use Google Photos rather than the gallery app that is built specifically for Android, since Android phones typically come with it already pre-installed on the home screen.

Google Photos allows you to access and share all your photos and videos from anywhere. After taking pictures and videos and uploading them to Google Photos, they become available on any device where you can access the service.

Benefits of Using Google Photos

Being one of the best Google apps and used by a large number of people worldwide, Google Photos is an ultimate benefit for smartphone users.

1. You get unlimited storage for free.

2. It works on all devices seamlessly.

3. You don't need to be overly tech-savvy to use Google Photos.

4. Google Photos comes with a variety of tools to edit your photos.

5. Photos that are stored on google photos highly maintain the original quality.

6. Google photos AI automatically detects the persons in the image.

Tip: The search option included in google photos is powerful and instrumental. It helps to get what you want within a moment from the huge amount of photos collected.

How to Access Google Photos

Having Google Photos downloaded on your phone serves the same function as a Gallery app. You can view your photos and videos from within the app, share them with other people, download photos from Google Photos, and upload photos via Backup and sync. You can choose to delete photos from your device or delete them from the platform entirely, all from your phone.

To access Google photos on your mobile phone

Open the Google Play Store (Android) or App Store (iOS) if you haven't done so already. Search for Google Photos and download it. After you have downloaded Google Photos, you can start accessing all of your photos and videos from it. Make sure you log into your Google account, which will allow you to access your photos and videos from anywhere.

Additionally, make sure to give Google Photos all of the necessary permissions. Go into your phone settings and select Apps and notifications. From there, find Google Photos and make sure it has the correct permissions for your files and media.

To access Google photos on your Mac/Windows

If you have uploaded or synced photos and videos from your phone to Google's servers, you can see and manage them from your computer. To do this, open a browser, go to the Google Photos website, and log in with your Google account.

From here, you can click on any photo or video to manage it. You can delete content here, upload photos and videos from your saved files, share things from Google Photos, and more.

Google Photo Interface

Some users are already seeing Google Photos' newly updated user interface, which makes it simpler to share several photographs at once or modify your collection without having to click on individual images.

The new change comes in a card along the bottom of the screen once you select an image. The card gives you quick access to features such as Share, Add to, Delete, Order Photo, Move to Archive, Delete from device, and more.

The update isn't appearing for everyone, but we've seen it on one of our devices and some Android Police readers who pointed out the change to us. It seems this is either a test for specific users, or it's changing but is gently rolling out to specific users. The change arrives on devices running Google Photos 5.96, but it's not part of a more extensive update.

This new modification to the user interface makes it simpler to edit and move photographs without having to leap right into them to make any changes. You have the ability to pick one picture or numerous photographs at once, which makes it simple for you to modify different aspects.

Upload Photos to Google Photos

The Google Photos app on your Android or iOS smartphone will perform the same duties as your Gallery app. The Google Photos app stores all of your captured media, including photos, videos, and screenshots.

In this particular instance, launch the browser on your mobile device and go to photos.google.com. Following this link will take you to the mobile page for Google Photos.

You should find a little Upload button in the top right corner of the Google Photos website. It's an upwards arrow with a horizontal bracket underneath it. Select this, and a small menu will open up, allowing you to choose the location of your content to send to Google Photos.

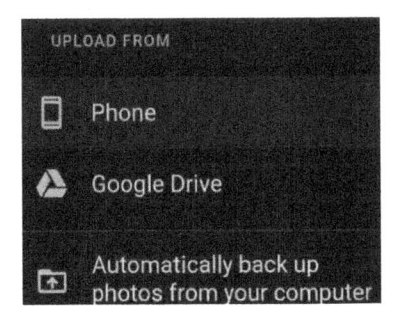

```
UPLOAD FROM

   Phone

   Google Drive

   Automatically back up
   photos from your computer
```

Select what you would like to upload, and then, if prompted, Choose your upload size. You can choose Original quality or Storage saver, which will reduce the quality slightly.

Press **Continue** to finish and upload your photo or video to Google Photos.

Download Google Photos

Most Android devices come preloaded with the Google Photos app. Whether you recently got a new phone or haven't used the Google Photos app yet, you can open the app and sign into your Gmail account. After signing in, you'll see all of your Google Photos in the app.

When you're ready to start downloading photos, do this:

Step 1: Open the Google Photos app on your Android device and tap the image you want to download. Then, tap the Menu icon in the upper right corner.

Step 2: Tap the Download icon.

Step 3: Verify that your photo is downloaded at the bottom of the screen.

Note: With only a few taps on the screen, Google Photos will download any stored images to your phone.

Creating an Album on Google Photo

1. On your computer, open photos.google.com.

2. Sign in to your Google Account.

3. On a photo, click Select.

4. Choose other photos that you want in your album.

5. At the top, click Add.

6. Select Album. New album.

7. Optional: Add a title to your new album.

8. Click Done.

Share Photos and Videos on Google Photo

1. On your mobile device, open the Google Photos app.

2. Sign in to your Google Account.

3. Select a photo, album, or video.

4. Tap Share.

5. Under "Send in Google Photos," select people to share with.

- Tap the name of the person you want to share with.
- Tap the Search button if you are looking for a certain person. Please include their full name, as well as their telephone number or email address.
- Choose multiple recipients if you want to share something with more than one person.
- Google makes suggestions about what other people should share based on your interactions with them to facilitate simpler sharing.

6. To share, tap Send.

Note: This will create an ongoing conversation thread where you and the people you have shared with can add additional photos, videos, comments, and likes over time.

Create a Shared Album on Google Photo

1. On your mobile device, open the Google Photos app.

2. Sign in to your Google Account.

3. At the bottom, tap Photos.

4. Select photos or videos for the album.

5. At the top, tap Add.

6. Tap Shared album.

7. Enter an album title.

8. When the album is complete, tap Share.

Back Up Photos with Google Photo

1. On your Android phone or tablet, open the Google Photos app.

2. Sign in to your Google Account.

3. At the top right, tap your Profile picture or Initial.

4. Tap Photos settings. Backup.

5. Under "Settings," tap Back up device folders.

6. Select the folders you want to back up.

Google Photo on Mobile Devices

Step 1: Download the app, then take a photo.

Install the Google Photos app.

After installing the app, take a photo of yourself or the setting around you.

Step 2: Find photos fast.

When you open the Google Photos app, you'll see all the photos and videos on your account.

Step 3: Edit photos & videos.

Step 4: Share your photo with someone.

- Let's take the picture you just modified and send it to a friend to see what they think of it.

- You should still be able to see the picture you just modified on your screen.
- At the bottom, tap Share.
- Select a contact, or create a new group to send in Google Photos.

Step 5: Delete blurry or unwanted photos.

Google Photos Vs Gallery

If you are an Android user, you are probably wondering what the difference is between Photos and Gallery on Android. Both of these apps have similar features, but they differ in some key areas. To begin, the gallery saves photographs on the local computer, making them accessible even when the gallery is closed. Photos, on the other hand, is Google's application for managing digital photographs and other images. Photos is a Google service that saves and shows photographs taken with any device that shares a Google account.

Lastly, both apps allow you to back up and share photos across different devices.

The main difference between Photos and Gallery on Android is that the former can store pictures and videos taken with your phone. While the latter lets you browse visual media on your Android device, Google's Photos app is tied to Picasa Web albums and Google+ social networking. If you prefer Google-based social networks, Photos may be the better option. But this depends on the type of images you have. Regardless of which version of Android you're running, you may find it convenient to save your photos in both places.

CHAPTER 9

Google Calendar And Gmail

Google Calendar

Google Calendar is a time management software application you can find on both mobile and desktop operating systems.

You can rapidly book meetings and events using Google Calendar, and you can also receive reminders about future activities so that you are constantly aware of what is coming up next. Because Calendar was made with teams in mind from the beginning, it is very simple to communicate your plans to others and to build several calendars that you and your colleagues can all reference simultaneously.

By taking advantage of Google Calendar's many features, you can easily manage and organize tasks and events in your schedule. Google Calendar is an invaluable tool for college students, company employees, business owners, event planners, and even stay-at-home wives. Not only can you keep yourself organized with Google Calendar, but you can also share your schedule with other users and invite them to your events.

What Is Google Calendar?

Google Calendar is an application that, like Evernote and Microsoft Outlook, can assist you in the process of creating written reminders for your job. It provides online calendar services that focus on easier management of meeting planning, birthday reminders, etc.

By using this app, you can access features that let you create event types, add event locations, send invitations, reset user permissions, add timeline tasks, sync with your Gmail account, and much more. Along with desktop systems, Google Calendar is also available on mobile platforms like Android and iOS.

As more and more businesses take their business online, Google Calendar has become a must-have tool for many. With native integrations with Google's apps, like Google Meet and Google Maps, you can easily manage and schedule meetings, organize daily tasks, and set reminders.

How To Access Google Calendar

1. On your computer, visit Google Calendar.

2. If you already have a Google Account, sign in. If you don't have one yet, click Create an account.

3. Once you sign in, you'll be taken to Google Calendar.

4. To change any of your settings, go to the top right corner and click Settings.

Google Calendar Interface

Google Calendar's interface is everything you'd expect from Google. It is simple, with Google's characteristic pastel blues and yellows, but it hides a lot of powerful features.

Quickly jump to different sections of your calendar by selecting a date. In the upper right corner, there are tabs to switch between day, week, month, the next four days, and agenda views. The main area shows the current view.

The top of the screen has links to other Google services you've registered for, so you could schedule an event and check the related spreadsheet in Google Drive or fire off a quick email from Gmail.

The left side of the screen lets you manage shared calendars and contacts, and the top of the screen offers a Google search of your calendars, so you can quickly find events by keyword search.

Add An Event to Your Calendar

To add an event, like a birthday, you just need to select a day-in-month view or an hour-in-a-day or week view. A dialog box points to the day or time and lets you quickly schedule the event.

1. On your Android phone or tablet, open the Calendar app.

2. Tap Create Event.

3. Optional: If you invite guests, add them to the event. Then, tap and drag the meeting block to a time that works for everyone.

4. Swipe up to edit event details like Title. Location.

5. Tap Save.

Change Your View of the Calendar

On your computer, open Google Calendar.

In the top right, choose a view: Day, Week, Month, Year, Schedule, or 4 days.

To Change view settings

1. Select the day of the week on which your calendar week begins, select a specialized view, and make use of a supplementary calendar.

2. Open up Google Calendar on your computer.

3. Locate the Settings Settings button in the upper right corner of the screen.

4. On the left-hand side, click the View options button.

5. Make your selections for the settings. Any changes you make will be stored immediately.

Important: The side-by-side calendars won't work for the week or month view in Google Calendar.

Editing and Deleting an Event

You can edit or delete any event on Google Calendar that you created earlier.

To Edit an Event on Google Calendar

Step 1: Open the Google Calendar app on your Android phone or tablet.

Step 2: Open the event you want to edit.

Step 3: Then tap on Edit.

Step 4: Now make changes to your event, then tap on Save.

Note: To move an event, drag and drop it to a new time and date on your calendar.

Delete an event

1. Open your Google Calendar from calendar.google.com.

2. Click the event on your calendar.

3. Click the trash can icon in the menu that appears. Your event will be removed and a confirmation message will be displayed at the

bottom of the browser window. You could also click "undo" to revert changes.

Note: If you're deleting a recurring event, you'll be prompted to delete all events in a series or a single event. You can choose to delete all of the events or the single occurrence you have selected.

To Create a Google Calendar

You can create calendars to keep track of different types of events.

1. On your computer, open Google Calendar.
2. On the left, next to "Other calendars," click Add other calendars Create new calendar.
3. Give your calendar a name and describe it.
4. Click Create calendar.
5. To share your calendar with particular individuals, click on it in the left bar of the navigation menu, then choose Share with specific people.

Tip: After you create and share a calendar, you can schedule events for that calendar.

Add Tasks and Reminders on Google Calendar

To Add Task

1. Open Google Calendar.

2. Choose Tasks from the list that appears to the left of "My calendars"

3. Pick one of the available choices by navigating to your calendar and selecting a free time. Click the Create button in the upper left corner.

4. Click Task.

5. Give your post a title and write a description of it.

6. Select one of the available lists from the drop-down menu to add the new job to a particular list.

7. Click the Save button.

To Add Reminder

1. Open Google Calendar.
2. Under "My Calendars," check Reminders.
3. In the top left, click Create.
4. In the pop-up box, click Reminder.
5. Type your reminder or choose a suggestion.
6. Choose a date, time, and frequency.
7. Click Save.

Tips for Google Calendars

Google Calendar has plenty of great features that can help you better manage your daily life. These are some tips you need to put in mind while using it

#1 Change your calendar view.

You may alter the way your calendar is displayed by selecting the tab labeled "Day" which is located just next to the settings icon. You will see a drop-down menu that gives you the option to pick daily, weekly, or monthly timetables, or even create your unique calendar.

Go to Settings, then View settings, and then choose "**Set custom view**" to create a personalized timetable. You have the option of selecting some days ranging from 2 days up to 4 weeks.

#2 Use 'Find a Time' & 'Suggested Times' when scheduling a meeting.

If you don't schedule your meetings on time, there's a good chance that people will cancel, or maybe even reschedule the meeting at a later date.

The easiest way to avoid these problems is by using the "Find a time" feature when creating an event. After selecting this option, the system will show you the schedules of every employee/client, as long as they use Google Calendar.

#3 Enable desktop notifications.

To avoid missing appointments, you can enable desktop notifications to remind you about your upcoming scheduled meetings. You can configure these notifications to alert you a few minutes before the meeting, or up to a few weeks.

To enable this, you need to:

- Click on the 'Settings' icon > Notification settings.
- Click on the 'Notifications' dropdown and select 'Desktop notifications'.
- You can also check the boxes to play notification sounds and notify you only if you've responded 'Yes' or 'Maybe' to an event.

#4 Enable Google Calendar notifications on Slack.

If your business uses Slack heavily, this tip would be extremely helpful. Similar to enabling desktop notifications, you're now enabling reminders on Slack. You can set a specific reminder time, say 1 minute before the meeting, and you'll be notified in a dedicated Slack Channel for Google Calendar.

To set it up:

- Log into Slack's web version and head to the Slack App directory here.
- Search for 'Google Calendar' and click on the app.
- Click 'Install' and 'Allow'.
- Choose your Google account and grant access to Slack.
- You'll then be redirected to your Slack workspace to set up automatic status updates and notifications. You can change or update

your preferences anytime by typing in /gcal in Slack.

#5 Set a 'Default Duration'

By default, Google Calendar sets a 60-minute duration for every meeting when you create one. However, you can change this to easily fit your schedule and shorten the types of meetings you create.

While you can manually change the timing when you create a meeting, this can be time-consuming if you create multiple similar meetings. Once you've changed this, every meeting you create will automatically reflect the duration you've chosen.

Gmail
What Is Gmail?

Google offers a free email service known as Gmail to its users. You can send and receive emails, block spam, create an address book, and carry out a variety of other fundamental email tasks using Gmail, which is comparable to other email services in many respects. However, it also has some other distinctive qualities, which contribute to the fact that it is one of the most widely used online email services.

How to Create Gmail Account

You will first need to sign up for a Google account before you can generate a Gmail address. You will be sent to the page where you may sign up for a Google account when you use Gmail. You are going to be asked for some very fundamental information such as your name, date of birth, gender, and location. In addition to that, you will have to decide on a name for your brand-new Gmail address. After you have successfully created an account, you will be able to immediately begin adding contacts and customizing your email settings.

To create an account:

1. Go to **www.gmail.com**.
2. Click **Create account**.
3. After that, the sign-up form will show up. Enter the needed information as directed by following the provided steps.
4. The next step is to authenticate your account by entering your phone number. Google ensures your safety by using a verification procedure that consists of two steps.
5. A verification code will be sent to your mobile device by Google in the form of a text message. Simply entering the code will finish the account verification process.
6. After that, you will be brought to a page where you may fill out a form with some of your personal information, such as your name and your birthdate.
7. Review Google's Terms of Service and Privacy Policy, then click I agree.

8. Your account will be created.

Gmail Interface

You will spend the majority of your time using the primary Gmail interface whenever you are working with Gmail. This window displays your inbox and provides access to a variety of other features, such as your contacts and the settings for your email account. In addition, if you use other Google services, like YouTube or Calendar, you will have access to those services at the very top of the Gmail window.

- **Gmail Drop-Down Menu**

You can access your Mail, Contacts List, and Tasks List using the drop-down menu that is available in Gmail. If you get disoriented while using Gmail, you can always choose the option to revert to the standard interface.

- **Search Box**

If you are having problems locating an essential email, you might begin entering the email's keywords into the search box to locate it.

- **Side Panel**

You can rapidly access your calendar, as well as create lists, make notes, and keep track of upcoming deadlines, using the side panel.

- **Left Menu Pane**

The left navigation pane gives you access to a variety of options, including the capability to create a new email, browse your mail, check your sent mail, and manage your labels.

- **Inbox**

Your inbox is where your received messages will appear. You can click a message to read it.

- **Labels**

You can arrange the messages in your inbox by using the labels. You are free to arrange your communications in whatever manner you see fit by making new labels and applying them to messages in any combination you want. You also have the option of using different colors for each of your labels, which will make them stand out.

Sending and Receiving Mails

Now that you've created a Gmail account, you can start sending email messages. Writing an email can be as simple as typing a message, or you can use text formatting, attachments, and a signature to customize your message.

To send an email:

In the left menu pane, click the Compose button.

The compose window will appear in the lower-right corner of the page.

You'll need to add one or more recipients to the To: field. You can do this by typing one or more email addresses, separated by commas, or you can click To to select recipients from your contacts, then click select.

Type a subject for the message.

In the body field, type your message. When you're done, click Send.

Note: If the person you are emailing is already one of your contacts, you can start typing that person's first name, last name, or email address, and Gmail will display the contact below the To: field. You can then press the Enter key to add the person to the To: field.

How to Print Email Messages
Managing Your Email

As you use email more and more, your inbox can become cluttered with old messages. It's important to keep your inbox organized so you can find messages when you need them. The simplest way to deal with email clutter is to delete unwanted messages. But you can also archive messages to move them out of your inbox, or you can apply labels to your messages based on the category they're in.

To delete a message:

- While viewing the message, click the Delete button.

Note: If the message is part of a conversation, the entire conversation will be deleted.

If you just want to delete one message in a conversation, click the drop-down arrow in the top-right corner of the message and select Delete this message.

Sometimes you may want to remove emails from your inbox, but you don't want to delete them. Gmail allows you to archive messages so they will no longer appear in your inbox. Because you can still access archived messages, it's a safer alternative to deleting.

To archive a message:

- While viewing the message, click the Archive button.

To view your archived messages:

- In the left menu pane, click the drop-down arrow and select All Mail.

Note: It will then display all of your messages, including archived messages and the messages in your inbox.

Creating a Filter

Filters can save you a lot of time by automatically performing actions like labeling or deleting messages as soon as they arrive in your inbox. You can create filters that look for a specific sender, recipient, subject, or specific words that are contained in the body of the email.

To create a filter:

Step 1: Open an email message. Ideally, this message should be similar to the emails you want to filter.

Step 2: Click the More actions button, then select Filter messages like these.

Step 3: In the box that appears, type one or more search criteria. One or more fields may already be filled in based on the email you opened, but you can edit the criteria if necessary. In this example, we're only looking for messages that are from Twitter. Click Create filter with this search to select actions you want to apply to the filter.

Step 4: Place a checkmark next to the desired action. If you want to apply a label, you'll need to choose the label from the drop-down menu.

Step 5: If you want to apply the filter to existing messages that meet the criteria, place a checkmark next to Also apply filter to matching conversations.

Step 6: Click Create Filter. In this example, the Twitter label will be applied to any new messages you receive from Twitter, as well as all of the existing ones.

Gmail Tips
#1 Selecting multiple emails

Let's say you have a large number of emails you'd like to delete. It would be fairly time-consuming to go through and individually delete each email. Fortunately, the majority of clients provide a function that enables users to select numerous emails at once. The majority of the time, they will appear as checkboxes to the right of each of your emails. In many clients, there is also a button labeled "**Select All**" that may be used to choose all of the emails shown on the screen.

When you have chosen which emails to process, you are free to take whatever action you choose, such as deleting, organizing, or archiving the messages.

#2 Creating groups

If you find yourself sending emails to the same people regularly, it might be a good idea to create a group. Many clients allow you to select various email addresses and save them as a single group. This way, you can simply select the group as the recipient instead of having to select each address. This feature can usually be accessed from the Contacts page of your email client.

#3 Email filters

When you're receiving a lot of emails daily, it can be difficult to keep them organized. Luckily, various email clients offer a feature called filters, which sort your emails into folders as you receive them.

You can construct filters that categorize your email based on a variety of criteria, such as certain senders or recipients, keywords in the subject or body, and attachments. For example, let's say you want to make sure emails from Twitter don't get lost among the rest of your messages. You could create a filter that sorts every email received from Twitter, as shown below.

CHAPTER 10

Other Google Apps

Google Meet

Google Meet is a video conferencing service from Google. It's a great solution for both individuals and businesses to meet on audio and video calls. It was born from Google Hangouts but boasts some unique features.

Google Meet is primarily designed as a way to host video meetings. However, you can enable the camera and microphone independently, so you can just use them for audio calls if you wish.

Anyone who has a Google Account may start a video meeting, invite up to one hundred others to join and talk for up to an hour during each meeting without paying any additional fees. See the plans and pricing for organizations for more information on extra services such as international dial-in numbers, recording and live streaming of meetings, and administrative controls.

Google Hangouts

This is Google's longest-running messaging and video chat service. Google Hangouts is a unified communications service that enables users to start and participate in text, phone, or video conversations, either one-on-one or with a group of other users. These chats may take place either in a one-on-one setting or in a group setting. Google+ and Gmail both come equipped with Hangouts, and mobile applications for the service are available for both iOS and Android smartphones.

Google Hangouts can also be a useful collaboration platform for enterprise customers. Hangouts also has an option called Google Hangouts on Air, which allows Google+ users to broadcast video calls live on YouTube. Hangouts on Air has gained traction as a free way for organizations to conduct online seminars and talk shows.

As of November 1, 2022, Google Hangouts is officially shut down with all aspects of this service migrated to Google Chat.

Google Chat

Google Chat is a communication service developed by Google. Initially designed for teams and business environments, it has since been made available for general consumers.

It was formerly known as Google Hangouts Chat, and it is a premium team chat service offered by Google as a component of Google Workspace. If you use Gmail with an email address associated with your organization, you are already a paying customer of Google Workspace, which means you have access to Chat. This application supports direct messaging, much like the consumer version of Hangouts, and it also provides threaded team channels, exactly as Slack does.

Google Classroom

Google Classroom is a free platform for blended learning that was designed by Google specifically for educational institutions to make it easier to create assignments, distribute them, and grade them. The major objective of Google Classroom is to simplify the process of file sharing between instructors and their respective classes of students.

Google Classroom is one of the most useful tools in the company service package. As its name suggests, it is especially focused on the educational sector.

Through the platform, teachers can assign homework that students will have to complete. In combination with services such as Google Meet, it allows a complete 'remote learning' experience via video call.

Google Contact

Google Contacts is one of the most widely used contact management tools out there. An essential part of Google's suite of web applications, it stores and organizes contact information, both for personal and professional purposes.

The majority of the time, Google Contacts operates in the background to help keep your Gmail contacts organized and up to date. But it's not just an address book: Google Contacts has evolved to offer multiple information fields and segmentation options to help you organize and manage your contact data, whether it's on your email inbox or even on your phone.

This makes it possible to organize and manage your contact information in a way that's both convenient and effective. You may manually create new contacts, change existing ones, and enhance existing ones in Google Contacts. Contacts can also be added automatically to Google Contacts from your Gmail account.

The first name, last name, job title, email address, phone number, and firm are all included in each contact record along with other fundamental pieces of data. You may also create labels and add comments to contacts, allowing you to organize your contacts in a manner that best suits your needs.

You can see an overview of all contacts, as well as contacts that are regularly contacted, other contacts, and contacts that may be merged or repaired, in addition to the labels that are being seen.

Google Maps

Google Maps is a free online map from Google. It's accessible through your web browser or as an app for mobile devices. You can use Google Maps to get step-by-step directions, find information about local businesses, and a whole lot more!

There are many things you can do with Google Maps, so let's first go over some basic features of the application and how to use them, then we'll look at some tips for using it effectively.

You can get to Google Maps by typing maps.google.com in your browser's address bar. You can also do a Google search for the name of a location or address, and a link to Google Maps will be at the top of the results.

Manipulating the map

On a computer, you may relocate the view to a different location by clicking and dragging the map with your mouse. On a mobile device, you may interact with it by touching it and dragging your finger.

On a computer, you can zoom in or out by clicking the plus and minus icons in the bottom right corner of the screen or by using the scroll wheel on your mouse. On mobile devices, you can pinch to zoom in or out of an image. This is how it works.

The Traffic button will display current traffic conditions. On a computer, this is in the overlay under the search bar, while on mobile devices it's in the menu.

Select a location by clicking anywhere on the map. Information about the spot you clicked will appear in an overlay. If there is a business or public facility at this location, the information displayed will include the address, hours of operation, photos, and reviews.

In addition to detailed satellite imagery, Google Maps features photographs taken from street level, known as Street View. These panoramic images allow you to see photographs from millions of miles of road in more than 40 countries. The next time you're having trouble figuring out how to make a slight right, try checking out Street View for a visual interpretation of the directions. You can also use Street View to take a virtual road trip and discover beautiful images of memorable places. Simply drag the pegman at the top of the zoom bar onto the map to enter Street View mode.

Google Chrome

Google Chrome is a web browser that has easy access to the internet. It was created by the same company that made the Google search engine. It is reliable, simple to use, and very fast for surfing the net.

Using Google Chrome is as easy as using the default web browser on your current computer (such as Internet Explorer, Edge, or Safari). When you want to visit a website or surf the net, you just have to type down the web address URL or link into the address bar at the top and press Enter/Go/Search.

Like other web browsers, Google Chrome includes basic browser features like a back button, forward button, refresh button, history, bookmarks, toolbar, and settings. Also like other browsers, Chrome includes an incognito mode, which allows you to browse privately without having your history, cookies, or site data tracked. It also includes an expansive library of plugins and extensions.

Made in the USA
Middletown, DE
28 October 2023

Made in the USA
Middletown, DE
28 October 2023